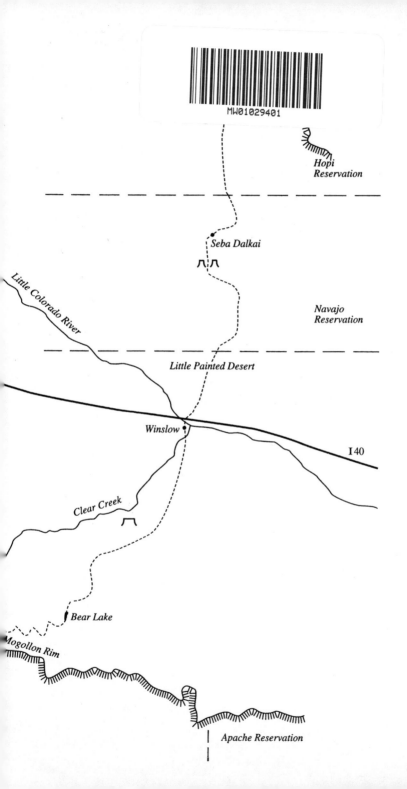

Hopi
Reservation

Seba Dalkai

Little Colorado River

Navajo
Reservation

Little Painted Desert

Winslow

I 40

Clear Creek

Bear Lake

Mogollon Rim

Apache Reservation

The Maze

Also by Lucy Rees

Wild Pony
Horse of Air
Take It to the Limit
The Horse's Mind
Keeping a Pony
Understanding Your Pony
Riding: The True Techniques

The Maze

A Desert Journey

LUCY REES

The Countryman Press
Woodstock, VT

Copyright © 1996 by Lucy Rees

All rights reserved. No part of this book may be reproduced in any form or by any electronic or mechanical means, including information storage and retrieval systems, without permission in writing from the publisher, except by a reviewer who may quote brief passages.

All of the characters in this book are fictitious, and any resemblance to actual persons, living or dead, is purely coincidental.

Library of Congress Cataloging-in-Publication Data

Rees, Lucy.
   The maze : a desert journey / Lucy Rees.
      p.   cm.
   ISBN 0-88150-369-x (alk. paper)
   1. Horsemanship—Arizona—Second Mesa (Mesa)
2. Labyrinths—Arizona—Second Mesa (Mesa) 3. Hopi
Mythology. 4. Hopi Indians—Antiquities. 5. Second Mesa
(Ariz. : Mesa)—Description and travel. 6. Second Mesa
(Ariz. : Mesa)—Antiquities. I. Title.
SF309.R392   1996
917.9104—dc20   95—39147
                                                              CIP

Published by The Countryman Press, Inc.
PO Box 175
Woodstock, Vermont 05091-0175.

Cover design by Trina Stahl

Printed in the United States of America
10 9 8 7 6 5 4 3 2 1

Rick
with love and thanks

# chapter one

JIM SIMPLY SHOOK his head. Like most true westerners he was tight-lipped anyway (it keeps the sand out of your teeth), and a cowboy's idea of respect is to stand back and let you learn from your mistakes. But he doubted we would live to do so: two greenhorns, the wrong horses, a long way over rough country, no pack mules, and, worst of all, no guns. This wasn't Whales. (They're conscientious about that 'h.')

Rick and I sat on the stoop of Jim's handmade timber house, our condemned horses tied to the fence, and watched the tumbleweed roll past over the wide valley floor. Jim resettled his hat with an air of finality and set his jaw. The oracle had been consulted, but its answer was unequivocal: there was a way to set about these things, but it was not the way we were proposing. There was no room for negotiation.

On this kind of journey, attitudes are polarized. You can treat it as a test of your organization and equipment, leaving little to chance; or your can trust in earth's bounty, your wits, and the odd bit of string. Jim, who organized pack trips for friends and customers, was both by tradition and inclination firmly of the former persuasion. While I, both from inclination and lack of organizational capacity, was firmly of the latter. Rick hits the happy medium of choosing his minimal equipment with great care, thus avoiding the ludicrous situations I sometimes find myself in. But care in choice implies a degree of pride in having made the right choice, a luxury of vulnerability we muddlers-through do without. Jim's vulnerable cowboy pride would not even have allowed him to formulate, let alone ask, Rick's question: "What would you think is essential?" You either knew or you did not go.

It was rather disappointing, but guaranteed to fire our sense of challenge. Out there was a land where Men Who Knew dared not go: a good traditional start.

Northern Arizona is vast and beautiful: "Like Wales stretched out tenfold," I had said to Rick. The rock is soft and young, blooming with the color and freshness of a ripe peach rather than the wrinkled durability of an ancient prune. Horizons are huge, for the dry air is so clear you can often see for eighty or a hundred miles. Mountains we would think to walk over in a day may be three days' hard ride away. There is space between each tuft of grass or cactus. There are lots of ways to die or become horribly uncomfortable, and nobody much to help you, for at least three-quarters of it is either desert, National Forest, or barren, sparsely populated Indian reservations: Navajo, Apache, Hopi. But the soul is at home among red rock canyons and sagebrush range; you can feel it running with the silvery-voiced coyotes when the moon is full, and this loosening of its attachment to your body makes death seem of less consequence. To be sure, the rattlesnakes, scorpions, drought, and torrential thunderstorms are there, and real, but they are less of a threat when spirit and perceptions are not confined, huddled in their customary defensive positions necessitated by a world of metal, glass, and walls. Or cowboy attitudes. The Hopi dance with rattlesnakes, knowing that it is fear that provokes attack.

In country like this, horses, our most ancient and companionable form of transport, are the best. You set the direction, and they work out the details; they carry the packs; they add their perceptions to your own; and their breath at dawn is warm and sweet. They like traveling; they enjoy the novelty and are grateful for your guidance. And their idea of friendship is to be in the same company day and night, week in, week out, not abandoned in field or stable and used when you see fit.

After three weeks or so on the trail, you are the leader of their herd, to be consulted, informed, accepted, resented, followed, trusted, and slept with, as a mother is with her child.

The problem, as anyone who has traveled with horses knows, comes at the end of the journey. Inevitably, you betray them unless you bring them home, which was out of the question for us. If betrayal seems too strong a word, an echo of soppy sentimentality, then try making a hard three-month journey with a horse, trusting your life to it, sharing an intimacy unknown even to most horsemen, and see whether you can feel decent about parting with it: if you can, I should not trust your friendship. Rick and I, who had both traveled with horses before, discussed this point more than any other in the brief three weeks between conceiving our plan and executing it. The only way I could imagine not being guilt-ridden afterward was to buy horses that were in some way temporarily incapable of finding themselves decent homes, and by traveling with them, render them safe, sensible, and affectionate. By definition they were to be the wrong horses for the job. The fact that we were too poor anyway to be able to afford the right ones was somehow beside the point.

Beside the point, too, was the fact that we had originally been aiming in the opposite direction, toward Mongolia, but had been deflected by forces beyond our control. But then, our whole passionate, pulsating five years together seem to have been driven by a force beyond our control, creating a kind of nuclear fusion whose brilliance astounds, baffles, and sometimes threatens to annihilate us. Traveler, dreamer, idealist, poet; doubter, mystic, self-castigator; funny, moody, charming, pigheaded, Rick is like Graves's cabbage-white butterfly: "Even the aerobatic swift/Has not his flying-crooked gift." The mating of butterflies on the wing is as chaotic and unlikely as it is inevitable.

"Anyway, they only eat boiled lamb," he consoled himself about Mongolia as we lay in bed one night. "And I like being able to talk to people."

"Australia?"

"Full of 'Strylians. Canada?"

"Full of midges, late summer."

"Arizona? You've got friends there, that's a help."

"As long as you don't mind that it's sort of one of my places."

He smiled. "I'm very fond of your places," he said, which concluded that phase of planning.

The linchpin of this goofy jaunt was Starr, a good friend and ever an enthusiastic supporter of lunacy, who lives in an alternative universe like a queen bee surrounded by a swarm of busy Chihuahuas, psychotic turkeys, and dreamy-eyed horses. There's a node somewhere north of Prescott through which the jet-lagged traveler may slip into a world of kindness and straight talking, hilarity, and apparently effortless production of small miracles. Camped in her twenty-acre paddock, we acclimatized to the high, dry air of Paulden's sweeping valley and picked her inventive brain. She took us to see various impossible horses, insisted on our buying a snakebite kit, supplied us with endless bits of information and help, and took us to the Prescott Livestock Sale.

There is something infinitely depressing about horse sales. While there is nothing inherently more awful about horses, rather than cows and sheep, being slaughtered for meat, the look of optimistic expectation on the faces of old horses that have always been treated kindly accuses the conscience. Puzzled, they scan the crowd for a friendly look; if you give them one, their relief in finding that their twenty-odd years of experience were not wrong after all, that we can go home now and it will be all right, infuriates you. They shamble over, stump-toothed, lump-jointed, incapable of retaining flesh or hair on their creaking frames, certain of a welcome. And people turn away ashamed, while the stockmen drive them in harshly to be sold at thirty-something cents a pound.

There were lots of them penned in the rising dust: stocky

old workhorses, a huge Percheron mule thoughtfully sucking his tongue, and some mad-eyed youngsters straight off the range. Nothing for us. I dragged Rick over to the cattle and admired the Texas longhorns, that disappearing old breed of long-backed, wild-horned spotted cattle that look like something off a Knossos frieze. Starr turned up with the meat

chihuahua

inspector, who was dressed in the western uniform of mustache, Stetson, long-sleeved checked shirt, belt with rodeo buckle, and dusty boots. One of the best things about the West is that it looks like it. The rough-hewn timber of the stockpens, the cowboys straddling the top bars, the steely look of eyes narrowed against a desert wind, the stockmen's whirling ropes: it only needed John Wayne to become a box-office classic.

"Butch here says he might have sump'n for you," Starr said.

"She's in the pen out back." Butch jerked his thumb over his shoulder.

"What's she like?"

"Hey, talk some more. I just love the way y'all talk."

Out back was a large pen enveloped in a cloud of dust. Zooming about in it was a *very* pretty little horse, stocky, spirited, and shocked. She shot up to me and demanded to be taken home, then zoomed off again.

"So why's she here, Butch?"

"Girl that owned her took off for California in a hurry; asked me to run her through the sale ring for her. I was kinda hopin' I might find someone who wanted her 'fore that. She's a half-Arabian, half-quarter horse—"

The mare hurtled up, rubbed herself frantically against me, pawed the dust, neighed furiously, and galloped off. One-eighth horse . . . But the brightness in her face, her short back, her strong, clean limbs, and the way she could "turn on a dime and give you a nickel change" were molten gold that merely needed fashioning. She would be fun.

"Guess she's a little upset. She's four years old, kinda green-broke, been a little overpetted, I guess . . ."

"How much?"

"Let's see, she'd kill out at about eight-fifty, so . . ." He consulted his calculator, added a bit for her having four legs and two eyes, a bit for himself, and came out with a price that would have bought a low-grade Shetland pony at home.

I found Starr sucking on a carton of chocolate milk.

"Starr, can you lend me some money?"

"You wanta soda?"

"No, I just bought a horse."

"Just like that? That little sorrel mare? Sure don't waste your time . . ."

I made Butch give me luck money back. In the days when horses cost tens of pounds rather than hundreds, luck money used to be half a crown or so. With inflation it has risen. I went back to the old principle that it should be a silver coin.

"You want *me* to give you a silver coin because I sold you a horse?"

"For luck, Butch. I've never bought a horse without luck on it. A quarter would do. Thanks."

"You Whales folk don't just talk strange."

I left him among a gaggle of swell-bellied ranchers, looking at the remaining coins in his hand and shaking his head. They pushed their hats back, scratched their pates, and gazed after me in wonder.

Rosie, my little desert Rose, was a spoiled brat. In most of

Arizona there are no fields; pastures large enough to provide grazing are too big to find your horse in, so many horses spend the working part of their lives in pens, being hand-fed. Rosie seemed never to have been out of one; but she had been loved. She reminded me of an overaffectionate puppy, sharing the same longing to climb into my arms whenever she saw anything new, which was often. Pop-eyed and puffing, she was endearing, exasperating, hilarious, and daft. She showed no alarm when I got on her, but I could feel she had not been ridden. Still, she was relaxed, interested, and willing: good as gold, bright as a button, and the wisdom would come.

Butch phoned us a couple of days later.

"How's your horse?"

"She's great. Doesn't know anything, but she's learning."

"Well, I've got one for your friend, maybe . . ."

She was long and classy, a limousine of a horse, too aristocratic to be pure quarter horse and, at five, a year older than baby Rose. Butch's Dobermans kept running at her heels in his little yard, making her dance about nervously.

"Saddlebred in her," said Starr, fixing her with a breeder's eye. "Tough. Comfortable." A short-backed horse like Rose is nippy but choppy in action; a long-backed one is easy riding.

I looked at Rick. He was lost. His own pony is a fireball, and he practically refuses to look at any other, let alone ride it. But this was a real lady of a horse, smooth, sensitive, creamy to ride despite her difficulties with the dogs, and her grace and beauty captivated him.

"Her eyes," he sighed, gazing into their soft, worried depths.

"B'longed to a rich college kid," said Butch. "Useta come home in the vacation and try roping off'n her. Ain't the type, though."

Bigger and heavier than Rose, she naturally cost more, but she was still ridiculously cheap. I should have been a bit more suspicious, especially when Butch proffered a half dollar and said he would take her back if she did not work out.

She was batty, of course. At first we thought she was merely highly strung, but she had a firm conviction, based no doubt on experience, that people were unpredictable, irascible, and painful. It made her unpredictable, hysterical, and dangerous. After a week spent trying to work out what panicked her, we could only infer that the college kid, infuriated by the Duchess's lack of talent as a farmhand, had hit her over the head, either with the rope or with his hand, from the right, when riding her.

People do hit horses, as they hit dogs, children, and each other. Using patience, tact, and imagination rather than violence in overcoming misunderstandings comes more naturally to some than others, though anyone with humility and a horse can learn. Some never do. They confine themselves to breeds such as quarter horses, which when battered tend to stop whatever they are doing and await the next demand. But the more sensitive types, like Duchess, become so terrorized by violence that, at the signs they suspect might precede it, their thoughts turn only to escape. To make matters worse, the horse's perception of danger is further fueled by tension on the part of a rider expecting explosions.

Duchess, then, would spin and leap hysterically to the left whenever she caught sight, out of the corner of her eye, of a movement on the right that might mean a blow was coming. It is surprising how long it takes to work out something so simple-sounding: it depended on where her eye was, as well as the size and speed of the moving object, the presence of ropes, her general state of alertness, Rick's nerves, and possibly even the time of the month. Sometimes she threw a fit when Rick was trying to get on, sometimes when he was trying to get off, and sometimes because her memory was sparked off by something we never managed to discern.

Journeys have a wonderful way of sorting out horses' neuroses: constantly facing the unknown together wins their trust. Duchess was sure to work it out in time. Whether we could survive the first few weeks together, though, became a matter of serious doubt. Mad horses, rattlesnakes, and cactus in rocky, fenceless desert make a combination as peaceful as juggling with nitroglycerin on a tightrope in a high wind. Rick's courage and determination in facing his and Duchess's fear of each other were admirable, foolhardy, or pigheaded. Starr advised sending her back to Butch; Jim, whom she justifiably regarded as thoroughly experienced in pack trips, simply shook his head and refused to discuss the matter further after he had failed to get back shoes on the poor demented creature; and I kept my fingers crossed. There is no arguing with Rick when he looks like that. His heart had gone out to his Duchess, and he refused to condemn her to the meat sale. *Amor vincit omnia.*

With these two idiotic animals we proposed to set out from the peaceful security of Starr's little ranch on a Quest. Proper journeys are not sightseeing tours, and tend not to be holidays; they are explorations of interior and exterior, revelations of unexpected terror and glory en route to some Holy Grail. Ours, aptly enough, was a maze.

On a rock near the cliffs not far from Tintagel, Cornwall, is a carving of a sevenfold circular maze. If you lay out its pathways on the ground and walk them, you are led round and round on parallel paths, deeper and deeper into the center whence, after a similar but reversed journey, you emerge once more. It is a slow burrowing into the heart of an enclosed, protected interior, an entry into, and rebirth from, the origin. In times of trouble it can have an exceedingly powerful effect—of concentrating your confused thoughts until the nub of the problem becomes clear, and then releasing you, refreshed and cleansed, to meet the world anew.

Like the paths of our lives, it is not straightforward. Time and again you are turned back on yourself; your journey brings false hope of early success before casting you further from the center around which you revolve; and emerging from its influence proves no easy task either.

How the maze got to that wave-lashed Cornish ravine, where Rick first became fascinated by it, is not known. That one is thought to be some three and a half thousand years old, though it may be much more recent. It turns up on ancient sites in Spain, India, Scotland, and Scandinavia, often as laid-out paths. In about 600 B.C. it appeared on Cretan coins found in Knossos, and hence is called the Cretan Maze. But if it represents the labyrinth in which Theseus confronted the inner monster, he needed no thread to guide him, for you cannot get lost in it: it is a process through which you are led, unless nerve fails and you turn back.

The Hopi, the "people of peace," are a Native American tribe, pueblo-dwellers, who say that we now inhabit the fourth of seven worlds, the previous three having been destroyed, as this one will also be, by varieties of man's stupidity and willfulness. Each world is less perfect than the last, yet each time we fail to live in harmony with its gifts. Only those who keep the tops of their heads open, acknowledging the spiritual forces that guide the processes of life, survive the destruction of each world to populate the next. After the last cataclysm, the Flood, the Hopi emerged in clans, directed to wander. Their clan signs and migration symbols are found on rocks, buildings, and kivas in abandoned settlements throughout both Americas. These kivas are ceremonial underground rooms reached by descending through a central hole in the roof, emergence from which symbolizes the reemergence after the Flood.

Some clans forgot their purpose and let their temporary settlements become cities; they became corrupt, and perished. But the clans that remained true were finally led to three barren mesas in northeast Arizona, a rocky, inhospitable, windswept desert plateau. Here they built villages, where they wait for the end of the world. They have a matriarchal society, deeply religious, refusing to shift from the values and practices they believe reflect and sustain the spiritual truth.

On a rock on the second mesa, Shipaulovi, they carved a sevenfold maze of the same complex Cretan design.

We had not known this when we went to Arizona; it leapt

out at us from a page in a bookshop, announcing itself as the purpose of our journey. We did not hope to solve the mystery of this convergence of ideas, though in itself it underlined the pressure people feel to make analogies, or models, as a scientist would term them, of the spiritual factors at work in our lives. In symbol and myth, as in the structure of organisms, function dictates form; and the pressure to provide a model of some exactitude, one whose truth will have the immediate impact that Rick had felt when he first saw the maze, will, like that of natural selection, sometimes hone that form into the same shape more than once. The eyes of octopuses and oxen are not only highly sophisticated but also remarkably similar, though they are built of wholly different embryological material. Fortunately you do not have to be able to understand embryology, or the properties of light, to be able to grow eyes and see; nor did we need to understand the origins of the maze to appreciate its symbolism. Mallory-like, we wanted to visit it simply because it was there.

Beyond our shared love of wild places, and this finishing point, we had a third, less clear purpose, a hidden agenda that only revealed itself as events unfolded. For we entered upon this journey in a spirit of exploration, knowing, as one might when entering the maze, that there was a center but uncertain as to what it was, or what it would reveal. We could not have guessed . . .

From Paulden to Hopi there are far more direct routes than the one we chose, but access to Holy Grails is seldom direct. We had to cross desert, a high plateau, and half Navajoland, which itself is bigger than Wales. Most of our route was dictated by the availability of water, a scarce commodity in Arizona; but where there is water there is generally something for horses to eat. We would wander along slowly, stopping where we were comfortable. We could carry about five or six days' rations for ourselves, but Starr offered to come and resupply us in various blank bits. It seemed a sensible enough plan to us; we were not out to break records or set ourselves endurance tests; but Jim just shook his head.

He had a word with the Fates, and they conspired against us. We found it hard to find another farrier who would be more sympathetic to Duchess's paranoia than he. She had an old but savage rope-burn scar on one back heel and would barely let us, let alone a stranger, handle that foot. Eventually we hit pay dirt: a German woman farrier who, comforting Duchess while the heavy dose of tranquilizer took effect, told us she had ridden from Canada to Texas on a Shetland–quarter horse pony, with a group of friends. Rick grew excited. Here at last was the technical advice he sought.

"Anything you'd specially advise us to take?"

"Goot boots."

"What?"

"You need goot boots. For the valking."

"We were aiming to ride, really."

"But first you must catch them. They can go far, when there are no fences. Even in hobbles they can go twenty-five miles in one night. I know." She smiled grimly, and reached for the troublesome foot.

The day before we were due to leave, Rick decided to work at Duchess's problem about being mounted. It is difficult enough to mount a tall horse encumbered by a bedroll behind the saddle; doing so in a strange place on a horse liable to think itself attacked is unattractive. He took her to the large back paddock, talked encouragingly to her, and got on and off several times. They were doing well; she tensed up but did not explode, until, as he swung up, one of the rivets holding the flange to which the girth attaches popped out. The saddle slipped; Duchess leaped; the second rivet popped, and the saddle, still carrying poor Rick, was catapulted several yards before hitting the ground. Army saddles (the best sort for long journeys) have a high metal hoop at the front, which hit Rick in the ribs; the rear hoop got his hip.

He crawled into Starr's trailer looking green and dusty.

"What happened?"

He told me sheepishly. "I thought it was the right thing to do."

I said: "It was, but it might have been better in a pen. When they know they can't take off they're less likely to try. Still, it was just bad luck about the rivets. Are you hurt?"

"Bruised my ribs. Took me hours to catch her: the Mexican boys from next door helped me. Be okay now."

Like many men with soothing, loving mothers, Rick had had a tendency to mistake colds for pneumonia, bruises for multiple fractures, and to assume that a mild whine would get him instant sympathy. I had been horrible to him about it for years. If I can't do something about suffering, I don't want to be made to feel guilty by constant reminders of it. Unfortunately I had trained him too well.

That night, as we lay in our tent under the juniper tree in the paddock, I heard the horses galloping, galloping, galloping. Half-asleep, I wondered idly why they were not making any progress. Galloping, galloping, never nearer or farther . . . I stuck my head out. No horses. But the noise, behind me now, went on. I got up. No horses, no noise. Lay down. Galloping.

It was his heart, clearly audible from two feet away.

Quashing my horror, I forced myself to think about that great resonating cavity of the chest, the organs in their tidy wrapped parcels. It had to be something to do with fluid from the bruising filling what should have been a space. He had not broken any ribs: we had checked that. I went to sleep listening to valves busily clacking open and shut, blood swooshing from chamber to chamber, the vast thump of the aortic surge, and marveling.

"Starr, you can hear his heart."

"Well, *good*; glad to know the old ticker's still lub-dubbin' away . . ."

We entered a strange phase, an eddy in time. Thunderstorms split the vast sky and inundated Paulden's golden plain, greening it overnight. Sheets of rain fell at random, so that neighbors on the scattered lots would say to each other, "See you had a fine rain today," while bemoaning their own parched dirt. The aluminum tent poles, objecting to being alternately baked and frozen in the high, thin air, snapped repeatedly. Dodging the black widow spiders in the workshop with audibly thumping heart, Rick patiently sawed and filed, riveted and hammered. Fortunately army saddles are designed to be mended miles from anywhere. Except when repairing equipment or cursing it, he was silent, immersing himself in his first encounter with Nintendo for hours on end until I hated bouncy little Mario with a vengeance.

Starr's father amused him too. A remarkably fit eighty-two-year-old cynic, he had been a gambler in Kansas City in its gun-totin' heyday of the thirties, and delighted in revealing the dubious backgrounds and dealings of people in power. "This country's run by a bunch of crooks!"

One of his heroes was Bill Williams, a Welshman after whom a nearby mountain was named. A big, redheaded man, gaunt and fearless, Bill had been a traveling preacher in Missouri in the early 1900s, and was sent as a missionary to convert Osage Indians; but it was they who converted him. He told them the story of Jonah and the whale. The Osage chief said gravely: "We have heard several white people talk, and lie; we know they lie; but this is the biggest lie we have ever heard," and walked out.

Bill began to wonder whether the teaching of his mother, an authority on the Bible, might after all be suspect. The religion of the Osage, who revered Sun, the life-giver; Moon, the ruler of propagation; Earth, the nourisher; and Thunder, the origin of rain, made sense to him in a way his own did not. He tore off his dog collar, married an Osage, and became a master trapper and hunter, discovering his spirit guide to be a bull elk.

For twenty years he lived in Arizona and New Mexico as an Indian, trapping, trading, raiding, and horse-thieving with the best of them. He also took to whiskey when he could;

and when he drank away the proceeds of his friends' furs on a trading visit to Santa Fe it was his downfall. Ashamed to return empty-handed, he joined Kit Carson in hunting Jicarilla Apache for bounty, though it was evident that his heart was not in it. But some Utes recognized Bill and killed him one night, sending the two Mexicans who were with him back to tell the tale. "We have no quarrel with you," they said, "for you were not our brothers."

The Paulden postmistress, too, was of Welsh origin. Her father, David Rees, was the son of a young woman whose family, passing through in a covered wagon, had, because of her beauty, been persuaded to stop. Rees became deputy sheriff of Jerome, a copper-mining town nearby, made himself un-popular with the chief of police and the mine owners by refusing to accept bribes to inform on his friends in the Wobblies (the Industrial Workers of the World), and finally was shot dead in a parking lot in 1933. Whether he was killed in the line of duty, or as a result of his political sympathies, was never clear, for the case was not investigated fully. He was a man with a brilliant, photographic memory, who loved sing-ing so much that he joined a church choir, though not the church itself. If he had to join a church, he said, it would be the Catholics', for then he could sin all week.

There was no shortage of churches to choose from. On the way into Prescott, not a large town, we passed the First Evan-gelical Free Church, the First Assembly of God, the First Christian Disciples of Christ (what were the others?), the First Church of Christ, Scientist, and the First Baptist. None claimed to be second, but there were also the plain Baptists, the Reorganized Church of Jesus Christ, the Community Church, Seventh-Day Adventists, Free Methodists, United Methodists, the Church of Christ the Nazarene, the Church of Christ, the Mile High Worship Center, and several more. It was not that we took the religious route to town: the Yellow Pages had a thick section devoted to hundreds more. There did not seem to be enough people in Prescott to provide them with a congregation of more than the requisite two or three each.

We, though, were going to the races, for Starr, who had been a show-horse trainer in Tucson before Reagan knocked the bottom out of the market by removing the tax exemption on horse expenses, had turned her talents to racehorses, and owned a couple. Neither was running, but we had to see the form. Most horses stay at the track during the season, surrounded by an encampment of workers, mostly Mexicans frolicking in flower-decked trailers. Chihuahuas bounded out to gum our ankles as we searched for Starr's friends. In the stands, the crowd held Stetsons and baseball caps reverently to their chests and sang, "Oh, say, can you see . . . ?" before asking for a blessing on the day's racing and scurrying to place their bets.

Most of the races were very short sprints; for the fourth race, a longer one, the starting gate was hauled around the other side of the track. But the ominous cloud that had hung over us all afternoon, lightning flickering around its edges, chose that moment to burst. Bolts of fire shot down among cascades of solid water.

Nobody turned a hair. They calmly loaded the horses into the metal cage, a lonely lightning-attractor in a huge, open space, barely visible through the waterfall. The computer board giving the odds went up in smoke with a loud crack; the announcer's voice was drowned by the thundering deluge; but it was time for the start anyway. The horses loped cautiously along, bumping blindly into each other; by the time they were halfway around they were all mud-brown, lolloping through a knee-deep flood to the lake where the finishing post stood bravely. Someone managed to jury-rig the odds board for the next race, by which time the flood had passed, taking most of the track's surface with it. The last races were skid-pan affairs, the horses slithering through steam like a Turkish bath as the sun reappeared. Somebody fell over, but nobody seemed to mind.

"Starr, this is crazy."

"Hell, Luce, track's got to make money. This is Amurica, you know."

We returned to our own sobering problems. I was trying to perfect baking bread in a little skillet over a fire, when I found myself watched by a charming round-headed insect, golden and heavy-bodied, who moved his head to and fro as he squinted at me. He was a child of the earth *(niña de la tierra)*, a kind of cricket that the Navajo call *who-seh-tsinni*, old-man-bald-head. He often came crawling around; when I picked him up he sighed and hid his great head in his front paws.

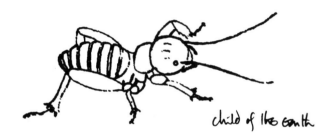

child of the earth

Duchess had a nervous breakdown. If saddles could ping off her, then there was nothing predictable in life. Rick would gaze at her sadly and return to Nintendo, while I fretted, my offers of help refused. When things are wrong, I tend to patch them as best I can and blunder on; he, a perfectionist, tears the whole structure down and rebuilds it.

"The bottom line's all wrong," he said one day, apropos of nothing; I knew he meant Duchess. "No idea of harmony. I've got to begin again, start from scratch."

"Pretend she knows nothing?"

"Yes. Let her run away until she's so fed up with it she decides to try trusting me. Chuck ropes at her until she realizes they don't hurt. Let saddles fall off her until she doesn't mind. What do you think?"

"It'll take time, but it'll work."

"I'm too sore to ride anyway."

When she was ready I got on her bareback, since I was sure that would be new. To our delight, she did behave exactly like an unbroken, but trusting, horse. She was genuinely learning what she thought was a whole new way; but when we put the saddle on her she thought she remembered, and doubts crept in. Well, it was progress, even if not a complete revolution.

I rode her up the broad valley, following the dry wash where the water came down in the rains. Farther up were gravel pits; the older ones, unworked now, held water where a million frogs burbled and splashed under the beady gaze of huge herons. They seemed content to watch. Flocks of waders, apparently turnstones and sandpipers, swooped in formation. I had never seen them dabbling in fresh water so far from the sea.

We waded through acres of wild sunflowers as high as my knee, heading again for the wash with its telltale line of willows. And suddenly there were so many butterflies that we could make no progress, could not see for orange gold fritillaries dancing before our eyes, landing on our eyelashes. Duchess was as astonished as I. I tried to find a bit of her I could stroke, but she was hoary with upfolded wings, and they covered my fingers. There was no sky; it was gold with butter. I do not know how long we stood, caressed by their gentle touch, shimmering statues intrigued by our attraction to those palpitating legs. Butterflies taste with their front feet; we were thoroughly savored. Duchess harrumphed indignantly as they tried to crawl up her nose, and we moved off. When I looked back there was no sign of them in the line of dreary, flood-smashed willows.

Duchess felt much less nervous well away from the corrals, and I persuaded Rick, now recovering when he wasn't blotto with Super Mario, to haul himself aboard again. We threaded our way through the trailer homes, with their wrecks of broken vehicles and broken dreams, that pimple the plain, and headed for the surrounding hills. We met a man in a pickup truck opening a fence gate on a dirt track; he offered us a beer and invited us to meet a friend.

Perched on a hillside, the friend's house was as sane as it was eccentric. Hand-built from local trees, it was the only one we had seen that belonged there. Most of Arizona's Anglo population are newcomers whose main idea seems to be to keep Arizona out. Bill, who came from one of the first settler families, had rather invited it to concentrate itself around him. Indian arrowheads, pretty stones and feathers, sketches and whittled sticks had congregated there. Instead of air-conditioning he had a balcony running around the upper floor; we lay in the breeze and watched rainclouds chase and collide, a bolt of lightning strike and send up a cloud of smoke. The rain smelled wonderful.

"Need it by now; it keeps missing us," said Bill. The whole house was supplied with water by the runoff from the roofs, and powered by the sun. Sunity, sanity, no wires.

In his forties, Bill had the previous year been on an artists' exchange to Russia, seen a woman across a crowded room, and fallen in love. Natasha had made it out only a fortnight before their baby boy was born. He gurgled in her arms. She radiated gentleness and calm joy while Bill expostulated about the changes that had come over his beloved valley: the filth, the trash, the wastage of energy and resources; the paranoia, the guns, the cocaine, the drinking.

"I used to fight it, but the only thing that talks is money. Look at it, this great country, and all they do is fuck it up." He turned to the baby, who gave him a radiant smile. "And look at him there. God, what have I done? What will it be like for him?"

We rode back in the dusk, passing a newly built house with black power lines running to it. Duchess stepped over them carefully, then leapt into the air, so that poor Rick caught it in the ribs again.

"What was that for, you loon?"

"Snakes, perhaps," I said, watching them anxiously, then found myself being bounced about like a Ping-Pong ball too.

Like Thurber's aunt, we were being attacked by leaking electricity. We kept to the open spaces after that, lit by a rising blood-orange moon, but two vast shadows arose to haze us: range horses, challenging our intrusion. Rosie chased them, snorting furiously, then pranced along, bouncy as a Superball, tail high, head cheekily turned to watch them following.

We got back to find that Gorbachev had been deposed by a coup of reactionary hard-liners.

Two days later, with Gorbachev reinstated, we set out, lolloping past the cheerful Mexicans at the far end of Starr's, under the railroad line where Rick had met his first rattlesnake and first tarantula within the same minute, and through the beanfields to the paved Chino Valley road.

Rosie gazed at the black stuff in disbelief. Ground should not look like that, glistening ominously and clanging against strangely iron-clad feet when you paw investigatively. Stiff-legged with terror, she stotted across it like a deer, leaped the white line with six feet to spare, and skidded to a halt in the opposite ditch before whirling around and snorting at it, while Rick and I cried with laughter. Poor Rose. But she was a game little soul, and came to relish novelty with the delight of a child at its first carnival.

Starr appeared in the truck, gave us our packs, and took brave photos of us outside the post office.

We turned off down a dirt track, passed a house or two, skirted a cattle grid, and were on our own. From here, we intended to follow the winding headwaters of the Verde River eastward down a gorge, but it would be a couple of days at least before we hit another settlement. A few miles down the track we went through a Texas gate, an openable section of fence, leading onto open range. Rick got off, and was leading Duchess up to me to hold for him to remount, when she erupted, knocked him over, and shot off, bucking wildly, the saddlebags banging against her sides. Damn.

We waited as she disappeared in a cloud of dust: horses usually come back, for they fear being alone in unknown territory. If you chase them, they keep going. She did not come back. If there were another track out, she would break her legs on the cattle grid; if she survived, she would hit the main road with its juggernauts. They do not stop . . . Rosie was screaming and fretting, so I gave her her head: horses can always find each other. We hurtled over a rise, to see Duchess haring along a droopy fence searching for a way out. She was still bucking. As we drew near she bucked around us in ever-decreasing circles.

"C'mon, Duchess, just come here and I'll sort it out." One of the saddlebags had flipped over her back, tipping the saddle crazily.

"Can't," she panted: "It's after me."

Soon she was galloping so close to me that I could reach out and catch her rein. Relieved, she stopped immediately. Often this kind of experience has a salutary effect on horses. They learn that it is always we who sort out their difficulties. In Duchess's case, though, it just unnerved her all over again.

Her mad bucking, and the weight of both saddlebags on one side, had cracked the wooden paddle on which the simple saddle rests. We trudged back to Starr's with our tails between our legs, imagining Jim's sardonic smile.

That night an unforecast great-grandaddy of all thunderstorms hit Paulden. We lay in the tent, hearing our luck change as hundreds of tons of water waged war above us, falling in cataracts to careen toward the Verde. Its normal tepid trickle would be raised to a raging twenty-foot torrent. If we'd been caught in the gorge . . . Flash floods, those walls of water coming from cloudbursts as far as a hundred miles away, can strike faster and more lethally than rattlesnakes, without even a polite warning.

It was back to black widows and Nintendo, retraining Duchess, and devising a system of straps that would hold the saddlebags in place even if she did go doolally. She tested it, with our encouragement. Even she had to admit it was safe.

I knew it would be all right when I found a psychedelic

grasshopper, an immature form with only buds for wings, decorated in outrageous scarlet, yellow, electric blue, and lime green; but I never found the peyote that must surely have been its staple diet.

Third time lucky . . .

 chapter two

IT WAS A BRIGHT, windy day, a day of promise and *joie de vivre*. Free of packs, we cantered merrily over rolling juniper-dotted slopes, gleefully pointing out the fresh, brilliant patches of grass by the washes. "Ain't nothin' to eat," Jim had objected. But his idea of a camping trip was to ride hard to some predestined point laden with supplies, set up camp, and hand-feed or pasture his string of horses. Ours was to travel light, stopping wherever there was enough grass for a bellyful. We were in no hurry: to us, this world was new, and we wanted time to enjoy it. Sure, there was no pasture, but there were enough pickings for two horses. For the first time our plans seemed not quite so fantastic.

The last week had driven me to a frenzy of frustration. Rick seemed interested in nothing but Nintendo, Starr was increasingly fatalistic ("Looks like this trip just ain't meant to be"), and I seemed out of step with the rest of humanity. But as we breasted a rise to see the deep green chasm of the Verde beyond the softly dropping range we were on, and the pink and yellow cliffs behind rising in serried ranks in a hazy blue sky, my heart bubbled. Here were space and freedom.

In the middle of nowhere we came across our first trace of mankind: a small, weather-beaten placard. THIS IS GOD'S COUN-TRY, it said. God seemed to welcome trespassers that day, though He had posted sentries to ensure that we watched our step. As we followed a cow trail down a slope, a rattlesnake

spoke from the bank beside us. The horses jumped, then
froze, peering cautiously about. But we could not see him: he
was too well camouflaged among the dusty stones. This, of
course, is the point of the rattle. Venom, being practically
pure protein, is biologically expensive material, too valuable
to waste on animals too big to swallow but heavy-footed
enough to harm a snake. If the rattle is ignored, the snake
can choose to inject only a small amount of venom rather
than inflicting a killing bite. Ranchers who had been bitten
said that if you keep still you spend a horrible, painful day,
but you do recover. It is not rattlesnakes, which have a
modicum of intelligence and choice, but scorpions, tiny,
deadly, and mechanically minded, that I fear.

We apologized to the bank, backed away, and rode on. As
we lost height, the scatterings of juniper disappeared and the
land grew more open, cut by ever-deepening washes heading
for the river.

Starr had arranged to meet us at the river at the end of the
day's ride. Like most Arizonans, she is obsessed by water and
wanted to picnic with us. We found an old set of corrals close
by the tree-shrouded, invisible river.

Although we had discovered most of the keys to her
eruptions, Duchess was still unpredictable, and I was concentrating too hard on Rick's leading her into the corral ahead
of me to notice a cattle dog that had materialized from nowhere. As Rosie peered doubtfully into the corral he leaped
to my aid and drove her on, nipping at her heels. She jumped
straight onto me, hitting the back calf of my leg with her
shoe with such force that had I not broken it at exactly that
spot some years before it would almost certainly have broken
then. Speechless with pain, I clung to Rick.

"What's up? Are you all right?"

"No! I love you so much it hurts!"

When Starr arrived I was sitting in the Verde's poor apol-
ogy for a river. Inches deep, muddy and sluggish now that the
flood had passed, it drooled through a shabby wasteland of
smashed willows.

"Isn't it wonderful? How I love this river!" Starr cried ecstatically.

"Gorgeous," I croaked, having learned that guests in America should never, never make unfavorable comparisons. We Welsh are rather spoiled about water, anyway.

"Holy shmoly, Luce, what've you done? Man, that's huge already. Well, I guess this trip just ain't meant to be. Lucky I've got the trailer—"

"We're not going back," I said firmly, crawled to the horsebox, and treated myself with racehorse liniment, horse dope, and beer. It felt great as long as I lay in the water. Iridescent dragonflies hung in midair to inspect me; a dipper whizzed by; a heron silently spied on me. Endogenous opiates, those shock-produced buffers to pain, added their bit, and I floated in bliss.

Terra-cotta, cooked earth: the red of kiln-fired clay, peasant pottery, bright brick; the red of the ocher that early men soaked the bodies of their dead in before the last great journey into the unknown; the red rock of landscapes of ancient dreams. Bushmen, aborigines, and Native Americans traveled for days, weeks, lifetimes, to inscribe traces of their identity, their clans, their wanderings, and their spirit guides on it. Alluvial sand, dropping grain by grain from slow-moving waters, comes in many shades, but it is red rock they seek out, for it is the lifeblood of the earth itself. Its color vibrates in the eye and reverberates deep inside. In brilliant light it mesmerizes you like a drug, leaping out from some chance outcrop to sink straight through the back of your retina and sing in your veins with the songs of earth's cycles.

In the rugged upland desert we now traversed, this glowing red, the clear blue of the sky, and the brilliant green of thornbushes rejuvenated by the last rains formed a magical triad of elemental colors that dazed and simplified us. This is id country: it teases the superego with worries about how well you are doing against rattlesnakes and cactus, desiccation and route-finding. Traveling this country with the top of your head closed takes a bristling armory of self-defense; but this is the landscape of our emergence, the terrain of our ancestors, the first paradisiacal garden of delights, and our evolution equipped us to deal with it. Its dangers are real enough, but if you strip off the layers of civilization and paranoia and keep the top of your head open you find, like my little hand-reared Rosie, that there is knowledge enough there. Coyote country.

Coyote figures strongly in every Native American tradition. He is the joker, the trickster, the one who teaches you through making a mockery of your pomp and presuppositions. He pops up in other cultures as the Wizard of Oz, Anansi, Gwydion the enchanter . . . True to form he appeared, grinning, russet as a fox from rolling, a piece of parched slope that suddenly condensed into life and equally suddenly dissolved, leaving us staring at a piece of parched slope.

It was Duchess who pointed him out. Horses' eyes are different from ours: not only is their field of vision huge, and mostly monocular, but they see movement far better, and detail far less well, than we do. They can see game at the moment it freezes, but are then uncertain what it is they are looking at, while we, following their line of vision, suddenly discern the camouflaged still shapes. When you have become a team they delight in stopping, staring intently, and waiting for the sign that says you, too, are alert, aware, and appreciative. Duchess turned out to be a superb game-spotter, pointing out distant deer, jackrabbits, coyotes, and, later, elk after elk. Rosie, puffing along like a toddler in her wake, busied herself more with which foot went after which on the rocky, almost invisible cow trails, or snorting at tiny lizards; but as we reached the top of each ridge she was astonished by the views, the sheer expanse of the world, and had to stop to gaze and gulp in wonder.

We were running about parallel to the Verde, avoiding the treacherous gorge itself, for there was still a danger of flash floods and we had no radio. It was craggy, broken country of soft, many-hued rock, often bearing the patterns of the swirling water that had first laid it down and then eroded it into the dust and pebbles beneath our feet.

There was little vegetation except for the odd mesquite—the sweet-scented, bean-bearing thorn of the West—a scattering of sagebrush, and, inevitably, cactus: little round pincushions and hedgehogs, taller branching staghorn, where raucous cactus wrens flitted, "jumping" cholla that fires bristly golf balls at you to hitch a lift as you pass, and the ubiquitous long-spined prickly pear, bright with knobbly red fruit. Rosie had not figured the stuff out yet. Phase one, whining about things biting her ankles, had given way to phase two, bearing it but sobbing at me to remove her furry anklets when I got off; phase three, recognizing the stuff coming, was as yet a mere predawn glimmer. But she was cheerful enough and I, frolicking like a salamander in the heat, was in seventh heaven.

Rick hated that heat. He found himself engaged in leading this frivolous cripple into a prickly blast furnace, a kind of unSuper Mario mounted on a time bomb. I could not stand, or walk; I could neither press baby Rose into the lead nor even keep her up with the regal stride in which Duchess seemed to relax best. He could not get off or on safely without my help; barbed-wire gates, though few, were fraught with disastrous memories. And the searing heat, which I adore, bothered him so much that he could not think.

That night we could not find the water we knew must be near. Crawling about in the dark, I nearly put my hand on a scorpion, the smallest and deadliest. Even that failed to rouse me from my strange bliss. There is a way of submitting to severe pain so that it no longer bothers you, but you do become dreamy and passive. From the way that it affects perception I suspect it is a consciously mediated enhancement of those opiates. Woozy and carefree, I delighted in the coveys of quail dashing for cover under mesquite bushes, the pulsating rawness of the red rock, and the rugged striped land laid out before us in waves as boundless as the ocean.

A yellow swallowtail butterfly, big as a handkerchief, fluttered after Rick for miles.

After a couple of days we came down into a huge, naked blood-red scoop where the trails became warm with the scent of cow dung. Upwash we found a big fenced stock tank. These excavated hollows collect the runoff in the rains, allowing cattle to be kept at the princely rate of four per square mile, and encouraging game. Scattering big-eared mule deer we turned the horses loose, filtered some of the gruesome tomato-soup water through the tail of my silk shirt (no lady should travel without one, courtesy of Oxfam: suitable for all kinds of dining), and boiled a kettle while Rick's butterfly delicately refreshed itself.

Duchess explored the water. Like many tame Arizona horses, she had possibly never seen more than a bucketful before. She sniffed, blew, pawed, splashing her belly and armpits in increasing delight. Yet it seemed to have some further use that eluded her. She returned several times, in between munching the lush grass on the sides. And then she knew. Buckling at the knees, she threw herself in wholesale, surprising herself before rolling wildly in a flurry of waves, heaving hippopotamus-like in a flowing coat of mud. When she'd finished, and shaken, and rolled in dry dust, and done the whole thing twice more for the sheer glory of it, she strolled away loose-limbed, moving in a rhythm quite different from her usual tense, stiff strut. Horses, like us, tie themselves in knots with their anxieties. For the first time we saw the inner horse, a joyful, serene beauty.

Voices. Impossible. But no, two cowboys came around the hill, behatted and bechapped. Two cow*people*. One was a woman, slim, pretty, and dark-eyed under her Stetson: Silke, a young rancher.

"Howdy. Y'all seen my cows?"

"They're the other side of the fence."

"Wal, shoot, ya gonna lie there all day, or what?"

We saddled up and helped drive the cows over country that grew more cracked by the minute. There were ten or so, a mixed bunch, part Hereford (named, a cowboy once told me authoritatively, after the well-known Texas breeder, Hrrfrrd), part Brahma, humpbacked and drought-resistant. They looked wild, but were docile enough. Rosie, who had probably never seen cattle before, yearned after them: she had already tried to climb the fence to get at them. Now she made little pounces toward them; within an hour she was chivying them along with intense concentration, nudging and nipping, turning back for a straggler, like a trained cow pony. But she was part quarter horse, evidently from a working strain. Like sheepdogs, these were selected for their instinctive desire to work cattle. It is not something that can be taught, though it is sharpened by training and use.

"Got a lot of cow in her," Jeff, Silke's boyfriend, said. "You selling her? Hey, no, not my hoss, you crazy mare. Stick to cows."

"Hoo! Hoo there, cows," Silke was calling. "That's not to scare them: it comforts them," she explained, between telling me the names of various plants: clumps of grayish winterfat, rabbitbrush, and yellow-flowered sagebrush, all of which are knee-high and uninspiring; Indian paintbrush flaring its scarlet trumpets from between the boulders of the dry creek bed we were scrambling down; chaparro or scrub oak, weedy and dripping with mistletoe; and little locoweed, which drives horses mad.

"Some people say it's like they've had a bad acid trip," Silke said. "They won't eat it fresh, but if they're hungry they take it dry, and once they do they get addicted. Then they're loco."

"How?"

"They act sort of normal, a little spaced-out maybe, and then they kinda bust out for no reason. They don't seem to know what they're doing."

"Do they recover?"

"No. Lead's the only cure. Right here." She tapped her forehead.

I began to wonder about Duchess. Was there, as we had desperately tried to figure out, method in her madness, or was she loco? I remembered seeing the blackened stalks of dry locoweed where we had camped one night, but she had not eaten it.

locoweed

It was a long, slow, hot trail to Silke's ranch, all ten hours of it. We wound up and down crumbly precipices, clattered and skidded down dry watercourses, came up over ridges to see half the world spread out before us in red and white stripes. The nearer we got to the river, the more deeply cut the canyons became, the sparser the vegetation. There were occasional little pools trapped in the rocks, but it was dry, dry, dry, and the bleached bones of cattle gleamed under the burning sky. Buzzards hung aloft, watching our tortuous progress as we picked our way down cliff faces and through boulder-strewn gullies.

By dusk we could smell the wet of the river; by nightfall we started to drop into the gorge, the air growing warmer and muggier. We slid down a mountainside into the black chasm of the Verde. Silke's hollers through the darkness comforted me as much as the cows, but when we reached level ground by the river they mysteriously stopped. Following the disappearing commotion, Rosie and I hit a head-high wall of tamarack brush, thick frondy stuff, found a little passageway, and crept along it until we met nothing. The ground disappeared; ahead there was only inky blackness, wet and foreboding. Everyone else had disappeared, too. No clues. I took a deep breath and urged Rosie on. She dithered, gathered herself into a ball, and launched into the void.

We seemed to fly for a long time. Rosie was a powerful little horse: the combination of massive quarter-horse rump and Arab springs gave bounce to her agility. We had time for aerial discussions before landing midstream in ankle-deep water and bounding on again. I caught sight of white water downstream. It was Jeff, splashing along contentedly. We crossed and recrossed the river several times, until I began to wonder whether this was some complicated cowboy joke for the initiation of greenhorns.

"What are we supposed to be doing?" I asked.

"Dunno," he said. "I never know with Silke. She sure gives you hell if you guess wrong, though."

Cowboy philosophy again. Keep your mouth shut, and larn. Unfortunately this means that unless advice is sought, involving loss of self-respect, a wiser man will let a fool beat hell out of his horse, or let his cattle die, without interfering. Judgment, though, is severe: " 'Bout as much use as tits on a boar hog" is one of the politer assessments of the ignorant. And "ignorant," like so many other common words, has connotations not immediately obvious to English English-speakers: it implies not merely a lack of knowledge, but willful, deliberate ignoring of lessons laid out for you. The knowledge is there: keeping your eyes open and your mouth shut is one of the marks of a good man.

Silke, at twenty-two, was trying to retain control over her dead father's ranch; the bank, either tired of the longstanding debts or doubtful of her ability to maintain the commitments, was angling to foreclose. On marginal land, in a declining industry, much depended on her being part of the usual farmers' network of exchanged information and help. To her constant irritation, she had to prove herself, to win the spurs that she had literally worn since childhood: her older brothers hated ranching, and she had been her father's right-hand man. But her youth, sex, and feistiness did nothing to win automatic respect.

"They just don't accept me," she said bitterly. "I have to fight every inch of the way. But I'm going to show them I'm every bit as good as Pop."

Like excavations of an ancient city, the little ranchhouse revealed layers of changing fortunes and cheerful hard work, its comforts not of luxury but of well-worn warmth. On the wall, a photo showed Pop on a horse, wholly concentrated on the cow he was roping, hand automatically but gently guiding his horse; one of its ears was on him, one on the cow, and it, too, wore a look of confident concentration on the job they were performing in total harmony. A powerful man, a hard one to follow, one of a fertile clan that had colonized this challenging land.

"Has she got more of a problem than a young man of her age?" I asked Jeff.

"I guess," he said. "Cowboys are still pretty old-fashioned about women. Guess there's not many jobs a woman can't do as well as a man, but a woman on a cow camp kinda changes things. Anyway, you know what they say—" edging toward the door with a wicked grin "—fuck 'em an' feed 'em beans; and if they don't like it, cut out the beans," and he whipped out to avoid Silke's whirlwind wrath.

We castrated bullocks the next day. Tired, we started late, in noonday heat. From her disgust at the way things turned out, I think Silke had been hoping to impress us with a show of efficiency, but it kept going wrong. Both the horses they had used the previous day were lame (I was secretly proud that our unfit, green horses had survived the crippling going unscathed); the first one she selected for Jeff from the milling bunch in the corral refused to pull back on the rope when he lassoed a bullock, and the second one bucked him off. She failed to rope the first time every time. To me, the skill involved in catching a scampering, dodging calf's two back feet in a noose and whipping them out from under him is awe-inspiring anyway, even at second try, particularly with an audience; but her standards were high. The job requires teamwork and slick timing, but I was too lame to help, and Rick had no idea what was happening at first. Silke's younger sister, Memi, looking like an innocent schoolgirl with her huge round glasses and angelic smile, ripped the balls out of the sweating beasts skillfully enough once they were held down correctly; but Silke was disgusted by the time it took.

"It isn't that I can't do it," she fumed as we fried up the "mountain oysters" the next morning, teasing the men about their sudden loss of appetite as they peered in the pan. "When Pop was alive, it all went like clockwork."

I said I was impressed anyway. The beasts had looked fine, healthy, stock to be proud of.

"But you don't understand; I gotta get it right, or I feel I'm letting Pop down. It's all I know, what I was raised for. It is my heritage." She was fiercely proud of it: her great-grandfather had been one of the first settlers from the East. Buying some land and homesteading the rest, he had controlled an area that, poring over maps, we calculated to be a rough triangle some sixty by sixty by forty miles. Her uncles and sister now ranched some of the better land; Silke's thirty sections (a section is a square mile) held up to a hundred head, a quarter of its earlier stocking rate. Legislation pushed by environmental groups in the seventies had cut the permitted numbers.

"Those environmentalists, they should get their facts right. They're just a bunch of Bambi freaks who don't understand how the land works, how grazing encourages different grasses. They think it'll all be covered in wildlife, but they even want to control the burns, so it just ends up choked with scrub, like Sycamore Canyon.

"See, a rancher knows how his country works . . . Oh, I wouldn't call myself a rancher yet, because I'm just on the edge of that knowledge. You've got to work land here for years, generations even, before you understand it. You aren't a rancher just because you own a ranch. Half these new-style ones, they're playing. They're just a bunch of goat-ropers with half the knowledge God gave a chicken. You can't make money at it. It'll feed you beef and beans and you can live in a shack, but the rest's hard work, dirt, sweat, and flies. The only satisfaction is from doing the work well."

"It feeds your soul, though," Rick said.

"It makes you feel like a person," Memi said thoughtfully, "out there on your own."

"You know where you are, and why, and what you have to do," Silke said. "You're related. So many people aren't related to this earth." Suddenly the fierceness left her, softening her frown and her voice.

"It's like looking on the face of God."

In the evening we drove ten miles to town and an overcooled bar, where our high spirits drew disapproving glances. The chromed mirrors and hard edges jarred senses that the desert's beauty had stripped of their protection. We surround ourselves, God knows why, with so much ugliness that we have to erect barriers of sense filters to survive without screaming. People were managing to ignore the cacophony of sound blaring from loudspeakers and clattering from reflective surfaces, the shrieking colors, the clinking and clashing, and were muttering quietly to each other; we savages shouted it down with stories of wild cows and bucking horses, leg-pulling and laughter.

At one in the morning they threw us out, whereupon Silke desired groceries. We went to a supermarket, an unpopulated couple of acres of shining tins in dazzling displays, mountains of vegetables, and parking lots of bread. Bewildered, Rick and I simultaneously collapsed, helpless with laughter. Our only explanations were vague wavings of arms, first at this cornucopia of complications, and then at the vastness of the empty country beyond, where the face of God is to be seen.

From northern Arizona, water travels hundreds of miles to the sea. Most of it is in a hurry, sluicing down chasms cut in the soft rock; but the Verde, once it emerges from its narrow upper canyon, is a lazy, winding river, and much of its water must be sucked up by the great cottonwood trees that dot its floodplain. Cottonwoods are fast-growing, white-wooded trees, with big heart-shaped leaves that clatter softly in a breeze. The bark is fibrous and shaggy, excellent kindling for a shady tea-break fire; but it is the fluffy seeds that give the cottonwood its name. As we plodded along the dirt road that followed the winding river south, these furry white caterpillars littered our path, wriggling in the breeze. Rosie snorted a warning at them, but, finding they ignored her, had to play hopscotch for ten miles.

The valley broadened, trapping the heat; opposite, the sprawling settlements of Cottonwood and Clarkdale blanketed the rolling edges of the floodplain, while above, on the hills, perched the neat old copper mining town of Jerome. We had explored it with Starr; it reminded me of a tight-packed mining village in the south Wales valleys, with which it indeed had strong links, for only best-quality Welsh anthracite was deemed good enough to fire its smelting furnaces. Abandoned early in the century, it had recently become colonized by artists charmed by the pretty wooden houses and the McDonald-less main street carved from the steep hillside: a paradoxically uncommercial end for one of Arizona's first industrial sites.

On our side of the river, the only settlement was Tuzigoot. Perched on a hump rising from the floodplain, Tuzigoot is a ruined pueblo of small stone-walled rooms crammed one on top of another. The guidebooks say it is an abandoned settlement of the Sinagua ("without water"), whom the Navajo, relative newcomers to Arizona, sometimes call the Anasazi, "the ones who went before." We hitched the horses to a thorn tree and joined the trail of flabby, pastel-clad tourists panting up the concrete paths to the ruins. The bushes were helpfully labeled: winterfat, sagebrush, rabbitbrush . . . Inside the thick stone walls the rooms were blissfully cool.

The little museum had archaeologists' reconstructions of brown people digging irrigation canals and growing corn. It is said that a combination of bad farming practice, deforestation, and ineradicable infestations of parasites must be the least implausible reason for the sudden abandonment of the site some six hundred years ago. The Sinagua, who seem to have disappeared without a trace, often abandoned a settlement after a couple of hundred years. The Southwest is dotted with these ruins: Chaco Canyon, Chelly, Betatakin, and scores more. There were exquisite little obsidian arrowheads, mystifying mummified macaws, and jewelry made of shells brought up from Mexico on routes that scientific research had taken years to uncover. The archaeologists admitted to many puzzles. Why bring little seashells a thousand miles over horrific desert to make jewelry when native copper pours down the hillside opposite? I wondered if they had ever asked the Hopi. One of the clans in Oraibi, on the third Hopi mesa, started its migrations in the south, the direction that symbolizes fertility, fruitfulness, and easy living. Its clan symbol is the merry, bright-feathered Parrot.

On our way south, Rick was having a hard time. The heat exhausted him, so that he could find no charm in the bluebirds that fluttered brilliantly around us, no interest in the landscape, no joy in traveling.

"How are you doing?" I asked.

"Practicing."

"For what?"

"Hell."

I felt hopelessly guilty at having dragged him to a climate that suited me much better than him. I had so wanted him to share my enjoyment of the desert, a desire that was not wholly altruistic since I found my own pleasure impaired by his lack of enthusiasm. We both grew entangled in a welter of irritation at being irritated, of guilt at our inadequacies. Hard journeys try friendships; being lovers who usually enjoy a deep and harmonious communication, we were even more sorely tried. I did not want to confess how much my hideously swollen leg hurt, any more than he liked revealing the misery mosquitoes caused him.

I am also being unfair. I did not realize how unstable Duchess felt. Although we had identified and circumvented some of the causes of her hysterical outbursts, her paranoia needed only the slightest spark to ignite into explosion. Knowing that his own tension increased her expectations, Rick blamed himself more than was just, becoming exasperated by what he considered his own inadequate horsemanship, and infuriated by his fears; yet he was determined to overcome them, and flatly refused to let me take her. Grim and gaunt, they pressed on into the stony heat, the flesh running off them in rivulets of sweat. I could only watch, and pity, and wish that my love and admiration could make more real difference, but they were alone.

roadrunner

We picked our way down the riverside where the floodplain was wide. Roadrunners flung themselves almost under the horses' feet. Avian Mad Hatters, they are quite as absurd as the cartoon character, raising their topknots in perplexity as they calculate the last second to dash across your path. They seem to live in a state of perpetual astonishment at getting through life in such disorganized style. It was strange to see them under the great cottonwoods where scarlet cardinals and mourning doves flitted, for they are desert cuckoos, living on lizards and snakes.

Where the floodplain narrowed, houses appeared, and we

forsook the lowlands for the desert hills above, losing sight of the straggling trailers. But the land had for the most part lost its charm. The red rock was gone, replaced by shades of dreary gray, and the heat bleached the color from the scrubby vegetation. We had no decent map, but by keeping to the tops of the rounded hills, which were bare of trees, we could set our direction well enough.

It was a long, long day, leaving us hungry in the dark, but we were heading for a friend of Silke's, so we kept on. Crossing a road, we heard horses neigh. A woman came out of a trailer and, seeing us, brought our horses alfalfa and water without being asked, as if it were a natural response to any nighttime stranger riding by. Such small casual kindnesses are one of the rewards of shoestring traveling, restoring one's faith in human nature. It was black when we headed onward.

Where the trails ran out we picked our way for hour after hour beneath a starless sky that grumbled and growled, navigating over wasteland by memory of maps and the occasional flickering of lightning over distant hills. The air was electric, the horses' manes charged with static. I dared not mention to Rick that this was precisely when rattlesnakes are liveliest, for he was happier now it was cool. Duchess came into her own, striding purposefully into the dark; Rosie, exhausted and bewildered, tripped along behind, whining like an over-tired child wanting its teddy bear, and my leg was too sore to urge her on.

I love riding in the dark. Horses seem far more alert at night, partly, perhaps, because of the ancient fear of preda-tors, but also because we need their gifts more. Without our superlative daylight vision we are rendered dependent on their more acute senses of smell, hearing, and vibration. At night, you can feel the vividness of their perceptions relayed to you, for they seem to realize that you need this informa-tion for your decisions, and even to be amused by the shift in the balance of your partnership. Rosie was too much of a baby to imagine I could need her; but Duchess rose superbly to the challenge. Tireless and magnificent, she paced onward for hour after hour, picking up game trails through brush and rock, warning us of unseen dangers and prickles with a side-cocked ear and graceful feint of her body, and triumphing when her explorations led us finally to a real trail.

We dropped down through a tortuous system of gullies that led into the dirt streets of Trailerville, that ubiquitous psoriasis of the Southwest, and got lost for hours. Except for savage guard dogs, everybody was locked up for the night, guns loaded against intruders, and all the streets seemed to curve back on themselves. At last we found a startled man in pajamas in a hedge, who to our mutual surprise knew Saartje, Silke's friend; but it was miles farther. Night riding loses its charms away from wilderness, and we plodded dejectedly along tarmac.

And then there was a car. An open sports car. Playing Vivaldi. And Saartje, a stranger, with a tray of cold grapes, slices of melon, selections of cheese, and beer, and an enveloping aura of laughter and life. We gave her the packs and jogged on, bareback, trailing her taillights. Rosie, revived by grapes and thoughts of her crib, followed the strains of Vivaldi, neighing when they disappeared.

Catalpa

We woke in an oasis, a lush green basin abundant with trees and flowers. Peacocks shrieked from a giant catalpa dripping with long beans; a parrot peered from a cypress tree, his absurdly brilliant colors camouflaging him among yellow roses, scarlet gladioli, and green leaves. Geese waddled over irrigated fields between an ancient blind Shetland pony and a couple of halt and maimed horses. It was a place of kindness, of joy in the profusion and beauty of life. Saartje collected pretty things and fashioned them into jewelry, toys, and what-have-yous: an earth mother on whom New York sophistication lay elegantly.

"I love your pony!" her daughter cried, bursting in after trying out Rosie in the field. "Will you sell her to me?"

"When I go home, if you'll wait," I said. I could not imagine a better home.

When I unwrapped my leg I was shocked. It looked like severe elephantiasis. From just below the knee heavy black rolls overhung a small rugby ball studded with five dead, white, immovable beans. Where Rosie had hit me was cracked tarmac, ominously oozing green. And it stank, unusually and powerfully.

As a child I was adventurous and headstrong. Fear of rebuke for the messy and inconvenient damage I did myself taught me to ignore pain and to respect my body's miraculous powers of recovery. If you don't panic, things heal just as well without publicity. But the stench, the colors, and the lack of feeling in this leg reminded me of accounts of trench warfare. Gangrene is still incurable. (Oh, don't be silly, it can't be gangrene. It can, you know. Twm Wern, the old shepherd, died of it after he cut his ingrowing toenail with his sheep knife, even after they took his leg off.)

"For heaven's sake," said Saartje when she saw it. "C'mon, it's the hospital for you."

"No, no, it'll be endless fuss and tests and days and days, and it's sixty miles away."

"The fire station, then."

Of course. Axes, ropes, lots of water. Remember the whiskey and the leather strap . . .

"Paramedics, you ass."

Nasty, he said. Big G not beyond the bounds of possibility. Try such-and-such cream, and if no certain improvement in two days, then the hospital for sure. He was clearly used to off-the-cuff consultations.

There could be no better place for rest and recuperation. Everywhere your eye fell was full of joy. Field theory, in physics, uses the concept of sinks and sources, areas or nodes where energy is emitted or absorbed. Depressives, like black holes, are sinks: they drain you without it having any noticeable effect on them. Saartje was a source. Could anything fester in such an atmosphere? Not my leg.

I moved a board to keep the peacocks out of our loft, turned it, and saw it was a picture. In one corner was a blazing, whirling sun; in the opposite bottom corner, verdant vegetation flourished, reaching, as plants do, for the light. But in the middle something was very wrong. Increasingly, the vegetation nearer the sun was more brittle, harsher, darker, until it formed an impenetrable barrier of death blotting out the source of light from its dependents, which would surely perish too. The sense of life and impending doom made my hair stand on end. I asked Saartje about it. She laughed. "Oh, that. It was a kind of experiment in automatic painting. I did it years ago, when I was young and unhappy."

But I had painted exactly that picture myself, in the same circumstances; and in rediscovering it I could feel again the sense of drowning in the city, of trying vainly to claw at what gave me life, bewildered at not understanding the blackness that was engulfing my soul; and smell again, Proust reversed, the dank brown wallpaper of my student digs.

Saartje's husband came in and threw himself into a chair, a giant of a man shuddering with shock. A boy they knew well had been killed at a riverside barbecue. It was purely accidental: a drunken lad had been fooling about with his gun and it had gone off, hitting the other boy. It seemed to underline the foolishness of guns being so readily available; but "the right to bear arms" is, as any American knows, embodied in the constitution. Only rarely can anyone quote the context. The Second Amendment (1791) states: "A well-regulated militia being necessary to the security of a free State, the right of the people to keep and bear arms shall not be infringed." The fourteen signatory states, unable to maintain a professional army large enough to defend their newly won independence, were to depend on a self-taught force of readily conscriptable citizens.

Two hundred years later, conditions have changed. Other outdated amendments, such as that prohibiting liquor, have been repealed, but this one seems hallowed; and, though no one could pretend that drunken horseplay with pistols equips anyone for modern warfare, the romance that the West is wild frontier country encourages the widespread carrying of guns. We had met people in Paulden who would not leave the house without guns strapped on their hips, and our refusal to arm ourselves had seemed to most people to be a mark of suicidal insanity.

The cream deodorized and deflated my leg a little, and we set out again a couple of days later, crossing a barren, uninhabited wasteland of gray gravel slopes dotted with creosote bushes. Of all types of desert, creosote country is perhaps the dreariest: mile after mile of waist-high bushes whose small, shiny leaves give off a scent of tar as you brush them.

Survival in the desert is less a question of outwitting competitors than of outwitting a biologically unfriendly environment. There is enough space, though neither soil nor ground cover to buffer the weather's violence. Desert plants and animals have ingenious tricks for surviving. Like the jimsonweed, desert gourd, or toad, you can mature incredibly fast after a rain, then bury yourself or your seed in a state of suspended animation to await the next one. Like a cactus, rattlesnake, or Gila monster, you can suck up water and grow fat while the going's good, then protect your stores savagely against raiders. Like sagebrush and mules, you can just hang in there in a withered, unenthusiastic sort of way. Paloverde, a green-skinned desert tree, has a unique ploy. It does not bother to put out leaves, through which moisture inevitably evaporates, unless there is a good deal of water around. Instead it stores chlorophyll, that magic transformer of sunlight into food, in its bark, which is a pale, almost luminous, smooth green skin. In the dry, the rest of it is an untidy mass of spiked bristles.

Paloverde is uncomfortable to gallop through without leather chaps, but there was no option after I let go of Duchess and for the second time watched her buck off out of sight. Exactly as before, we had just come through a Texas gate, but this time it was I who was holding her. Perhaps it was the mere similarity of the situation that set her off, though we had been through numerous fences since the first time; or perhaps we had made the first circle of our maze and arrived back in a parallel position. "In any given situation the animal tends to do exactly what it did last time," one animal psychologist put it. Duchess complied, bucking away and failing to reappear. She did not care for Rose, or us: she wanted out. Rosie and I tore through the brush and found her half a mile down the fence, far more unscathed than we; the rigging had kept everything in place.

Rick felt marginally better that I, too, let go of horses, but it made him wonder uncertainly whether I was as infallible a horsewoman as he had assumed. "These things happen," I said, picking inch-long paloverde thorns out of my stinging flesh.

"Yeah, *when?*"

Desolate hills stretched for mile after mile in pitiless heat. Our map was no good, for it showed only roads, which we did not want. The bits we traversed were blank. We held steadily south-southeast, sometimes picking up a jeep track but more often trudging through gravel or fighting our way through paloverde-choked gullies.

We dropped down blindly off the hills into a car-wrecker's yard. It was closed, but there was water; and immediately below it, miraculously, was the hollow where Joe lived. We had met him several days earlier, on a dirt road in the middle of nowhere, refilling our water bottles from the tank in the back of his pickup. His trailer was shaded by a magnificent cottonwood and surrounded by real grass, ankle-deep and green. Gratefully clutching a cold beer, I hit the deck; but for Joe the underswell of rest-day drinking kept the deck in perpetual motion. His skilled negotiation of its tilts and lurches added to the charm of his conversation.

Part Cherokee, Joe had no particular desire to enter any rat race. A roof, a beer, a shade tree, and the wide land he traveled were enough, though when he showed us the photographs of the children his wife had taken away when she left him, the puzzled hurt in his eyes brought tears to mine. Yet his gentle acceptance of the world's quirks seemed complete. Starr, who turned up with a truckful of goodies and made herself at home preparing steaks while we sprawled lazily, was equally charmed: "Where do you *find* these wonderful people?"

We watched videos until early morning. I asked Joe what he did.

"Construction." He laughed. "In fact, I seem to spend most of my time wrecking things. Construction, destruction, it's all the same."

Horses and roads do not mix well, but we found it hard to avoid a long-drawn-out suburbia straggling southward along the river. Here, it was my underlying terror about the incompatibility of soft flesh and hurtling metal that gave rise to irritation. Drivers can be singularly stupid; Rosie was pop-eyed with horror about dogs, signs, flags, and mailboxes, practicing her sideways jack-in-the-box technique to perfection; there really was no food or water, and the few occupied houses we passed offered only blank, xenophobic stares. The shoulders were littered with broken glass and tins, and the views obliterated by festoons of overhead wires. I have never understood why people move to a beautiful place and instantly destroy what brought them there. Arizona has less excuse than most states, for the legacy of the old Spanish adobe buildings provides a model for cool, gracious living, even on a small scale. I fumed at the obscenity of carefully tended golf courses steaming in the heat; but Duchess sailed along serenely, and Rick relaxed. Finally we emerged into an orange desert.

Montezuma Well, like Montezuma Castle, a ruined pueblo several miles away, has nothing to do with Montezuma. The term simply implies age and Indians, though it seemed disdainfully *ignorant* to me. It is a huge, sheer-sided hole in an otherwise fairly featureless plain, some fifty-five feet deep, with brilliant green water at the bottom. The narrow band of grass fringing the water was almost unbearably lush; I wondered how we could get the horses down, but the paths were too narrow to allow us to pass the shuffling septuagenarians clutching pamphlets and cameras. There were tiny houses in a pocket high in the cliff wall, and others nearby; their inhabitants had laced the plain with an extensive irrigation system, at which the tourists marveled. I was fascinated by their fascination in the remains of a culture their values had destroyed. The only good Indian is a dead Indian, it seems.

A woman in a white cotton sunhat from Seattle lectured me on survival in the desert. She and her husband had driven from the Grand Canyon in the last two days, so she knew a good deal that would be useful to me. There wasn't any water, and it could get hot; moreover, there were dangerous rattlesnakes. I stared at her white socks, nodding dutifully, before saddling up and galloping off in a cloud of red dust, howling.

We were heading for cliffs over a flat red desert, alone at last but for the quail and cottontails scuttling from under our feet. Desert quail have a strange blob of a comb growing from the tops of their heads and overhanging their beaks, so they look like donkeys chasing their own carrots. The desert was alive with them, for the soft rust-red sand was richly verdant: ancient gnarled mesquite, whose beans the horses plucked and munched as they passed by; desert acacia, whose perfumed yellow balls of flowers scent the spring; barrel cactus, with wicked fishhooks of spines protecting the sweet water within; ocatilla, whose tall dead stems, long skates' tails of thorns, split open after a rain to exude tiny leaves surmounted by the scarlet trumpets beloved of hummingbirds. In the evening, in slanting sunlight, the red earth pulsated like a beating heart, the greens luminous against it. We strode on, glowing, our etiolated shadows preceding us as we turned east. Ahead loomed the rim of a vast plateau, a promise of cool, unpopulated unknown. Harmony pervaded our souls.

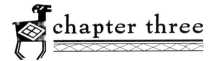

chapter three

MOST OF NORTHERN Arizona is an enormous uplifted bulge, through which the Grand Canyon cuts a deep slash that reveals the layers of its anatomy. At its southern edge, the Mogollon Rim, the plateau stops abruptly in a wall of sheer cliffs; its western edge, which we were now approaching, is shattered by a series of tree-lined canyons and clear-running creeks cutting deep into the red rock: Sycamore Canyon, Oak Creek, and Sedona, the mecca of the drifting lost, earnestly dissecting their innards in pursuit of essences that cannot be found in burgeoning stores, however "spiritual" their wares.

Far from such complications, we pursued simpler essences: food for the horses, and water. A dirt track led us to Beaver Creek, at the bottom of the cliffs. In the dark we passed the huts of a ranger station, then a fence that enclosed shaggy and sweet-smelling vegetation.

"Grass! A field!" It was about as likely as finding an ice-cream cactus. But it was theirs, we reflected sadly; we'd have to find our own. There was a campground. Normally I hate them, but treasure a soft spot for National Forest campsites. To me, they embody that deep-rooted American sense of democracy that subtly pervades all that is best in that great country. Oh, I know you can crab about those who for reasons of color or poverty are debarred, about the apparently inevitable corruptions owing to power politics and big money, about the cynicism and the crime, the naiveté and self-congratulation, but listen:

In Britain, ordinary people say: "It's a disgrace. They ought to do something about it."

In America, ordinary people say: "We've a ways to go yet, but we're working on it."

National Forest is public land. *Our* land, any American would say: yours and mine to appreciate and enjoy. We didn't keep it out of private hands to be regulated by a bunch of bureaucratic tyrants. So how would we like our campsites? Well, we'd like to feel the immensity of the wilderness without its hardships and dangers, so we'd like private sites, isolated from each other, but not too far from a central washhouse. We love campfires, but we acknowledge there's a risk, so we'll each have a barbecue pit: handy to fix a grill there, too. We'd like notices that invite you into a sense of shared responsibility and understanding rather than lists of vetoes. We don't like rules much, or monitors either, but we'd like someone on hand to advise us if things should go wrong.

Welcome to Beaver Creek campsite, one of a million.

We doubled back to the ranger station to ask about the horses. "Say now," said Ranger Roy through a mouthful of supper, "we've got a field; it's stirrup-high in grass. Guess we've got oats, too. Good to see you."

I opened up a can of deviled ham that night to have with our rice, and since the bare earth of our site was a scorpion-free zone, we rolled out the bedding under the stars. I woke with Rick's elbow in my ribs. Metal rattled.

"What's that?" He pointed the torch beam. Just beyond our feet shimmered a white plume, flamboyant as an ostrich feather.

"Oh God, a skunk. That can."

"Shoo! Piss off!" he cried, kicking. The tail flicked ominously at us.

"Rick!" I hissed, clutching him. *"You don't say that to*

skunks. Please, Mr. Skunk, sir, forgive my friend in his ignorance . . ."

"I'm not going to be held ransom by a furry rat."

"You are, you know."

Of all possible ignominious endings to our expedition, I
hadn't envisaged being skunked out. Skunk spray is un-
imaginably potent. The liquid rotting carcasses that dogs
delight to roll in, old vomit, hedgehog farts, or putrifying
chicken guts only hint at it, as an acorn hints at the magnificent architecture of an oak tree. A skunk's aim is more accurate, more arresting, than that of a Colt .45. Anything it
sprays, you burn, with apologies to the county.

We had no complete change of clothes.

Giggling with horror, we watched as he threatened our
entire wardrobe, flounced about, cleaned out the can, and
strolled off. A moment later a bigger one appeared. The first
came back. They argued over possession of the can. They
faced, or rather, bottomed, each other across our feet, chittering,
tail-flicking, stamping, and jumping. When they ran off I
stuffed the spotless can in my saddlebag, rolled it up, and put
it under my leg, which appreciated the elevation. All night
I kept reawakening to furious burrowings under my foot;
little hands pulled at me, and teeth gnawed in vain.

In the morning a deer strolled up to me.

Rick felt good. Cool, cactus-free country ahead, well-fed
horses, and a deliciously blank map: what more could a
traveler want? He went over to the next site with the offend-
ing can while I went for the horses.

"Would you mind taking this out for us? We're on horseback and we don't want to carry litter, but I don't want to
leave it, either."

"Oh, you're English! Well, what d'you know? Of course
we'll take it. On horses? Gee, that's great; what a way to
travel. Where are they now?"

"My lady's just gone to get them."

Arriving, I said: "You're not going to believe this . . ."

He's quick. I watched him realize, watched the realization bounce through a spectrum of emotions, watched him catch Coyote by the tail; he turned back to the woman with scarcely a pause, waving his hand over a hundred miles of desert. "Oh, out there."

Roy lent us a pickup, another ranger, and a bucket of oats, and we set off the way we'd come. Horses backtrack, preferring the devil they know. Luckily we had passed a cattle grid, so they could not get back to Joe's. But they had remembered the grid and had turned off up a trail running in the same direction. It was easy tracking them in the dusty stones; they had held their direction for five miles before hitting a fence. Picking at a juniper bush, they looked awful, as well they might after a hungry, thirsty, sleepless night. Rosie was astonished at the coincidence of our meeting in the middle of nowhere. She had scratched herself knocking the fence down, the fool.

We fed them, and saddled up. They felt exhausted, finished before the day had started. But an hour farther down Beaver Creek we found a patch of vivid green grass growing out of clear running water. A fish eagle rose with a mighty effort and flapped away through the trees. We lit a fire and made a long-delayed breakfast while the horses rehydrated. There would be no moving for a couple of hours. We started to laugh.

From across the stream, a track zigzagged up the side of a steep 1500-foot slope. The map claims it is negotiable with four-wheel drive, but you'd need a lot of nerve and skill, too, and evidently nobody had tried recently. We rose above the rolling red desert where dust-devils chased their tails, and ascended into heaven.

In heaven the sun shines from a blue, blue sky, but it is never too hot, and there are no flies. A continuous light breeze ripples the golden-flowering sagebrush, so that the wide sweeps of land undulate like a slow swell at sea. From between the stones, drifts of little flowers, pink, white, yellow, and blue, congregate in shifts of shade and aroma. Rosie's white socks are splattered with red, yet even blood isn't blood here, but tiny berries. Juniper and scrub oak darken some rises, offering cover to herds of sleekly fat elk. And being heaven, it's infinite, singing in the high breeze.

We wandered over the plateau, shedding tensions like unwanted cactus prickles. The map, speckled with names like Cedar Flat, Deadwood Draw, Maverick Butte, and Wild Horse Mesa, bore no relation to the long swoops of gold or green, the nipples of peppercorn rock, the moving hillsides of elk; the trails were transitory illusions anyhow. How fast we were moving, or how much time had elapsed, were questions the mind refused to consider in clouds of cerulean butterflies. When we needed water, we would come to a tank soon after; if we needed grass, it would be a fenced tank; when night fell there was a huge tank surrounded by little paddocks fertilized by cattle. But there was no sign of anyone, or of cattle; we might have been in the middle of the ocean.

It is for days like this that we travel, days of feeling wholly at one with land yet newly discovered; perhaps previous days of privation and disharmony enhance them, as hunger enhances the pleasure of eating. Getting there under your own steam is necessary, too, for the rhythm of movement loosens your thoughts. *The great affair is to move,* as Stevenson said. Once movement has become automatic, especially in slow-changing, vast-skied land, you submerge into an unthinking, unfeeling unconscious that links the roots of thought and emotion without distinction. Anyone who is fluent in more than one language knows that you rarely translate from one to another; rather, you translate the precursors of expression from a formless pre-language into the concrete identifications of one particular language, and the characteristic structure and vocabulary of that language impose a structure on your thoughts.

Similarly there is a state of being that precedes thought and feeling, often, alas, so distinct and separate: pre-thought, pre-emotion, the unconscious itself. By definition it is almost unreachable, yet I believe that it is there that we visit in these conditions, and in the same way that it is almost impossible to describe the impact of a dream to any satisfaction, it is almost impossible to say what goes on then. There are no conclusions, no revelations, yet the internal architecture of the self is allowed an airing, with the opportunity for reorganization. On emerging from such a state to grapple with more mundane realities, you feel as if you have been in a trance, or drugged; you cannot say what you have been thinking; but later, maybe even months later, you may find that the superstructure of your attitudes has been torn down and rebuilt from subtly altered foundations, and you immediately identify the point at which it happened with great sureness and clarity, although no such effect was clear at the time.

What is clear is perception itself, perception liberated from the filters of attention and search image to assault you with rare intensity. I remember the shine on the eye of a lizard, the exact shade of pink of a little thriftlike flower, the high-toned singing of the breeze, with utmost vividness. As for revelations: nothing dramatic. I was at home, and happy.

Duchess loved that open plateau. We dismounted and walked for hours, Rick and she striding ahead long-legged and easy together, I puttering behind with my naturalist's intrigues, feeling the circulation returning to my leg. I turned Rosie loose. She scampered about like a puppy, munching here, chasing butterflies there, cheekily dodging me lest I catch her again.

Many people consider discipline and physical restraint the keystones to managing a horse. "Teach the horse who's master: don't let him get away with it." Horses certainly learn to avoid pain, but whether they understand the concept of master, or of outwitting authority, is another matter, and one that reaches as deep into our evolution as theirs.

Primate societies, and most human ones, are often based on a hierarchical system ruled by an alpha male (or honorary male) whose bullying edicts give rise to scheming and power struggles in the ranks below. It is a pattern repeated among carnivores that, although potentially lethal to each other, need to come together for cooperative hunting. The strong arm rules; might is right; and *lèse-majesté* prevails. It is not the only human social pattern, but it is one that we and dogs intuitively recognize.

Horses do not. They come together for security, and what keeps them together is love, the bonds of friendship and family we also recognize. Their stallion is not their lord and master, but their guardian and mate. He is seldom even their leader: she is some wise old mare whose judgment they follow. A horse gives you his loyalty because your steadfast good sense, especially at times when his small courage fails him, impresses him, not because you dominate him. If you are safe and unafraid, he wants to be in the same place.

Our difficulty in understanding this fundamental difference between the psychology of the hunter and that of the hunted is striking, so much so that it makes me wonder how much instinct lurks beneath our attitudes. We set up contests of will between ourselves and our horses, and become anxious when we seem to be losing, interpreting the horse's natural exuberance as disobedience. We set up contests between them, too, giving them buckets of food to squabble over and noting in self-justification that they also have bullies and subordinates. We fail to note that in the wild they have nothing to compete over, nor that the bully stands apart from the group in the field. Given the choice, horses avoid bullies.

We seldom give them the choice. We have clever methods of restraint, designed to hurt if they make a wrong move. With a certain sweetening of cajolery, reward, and kindness, they learn to do what we ask. It is ironic that our usual way of dealing with that archetype of the free spirit is by threatening it with pain.

> He who binds to himself a joy
> Doth the winged life destroy.

If we, with our infinitely superior intelligence and imagination, cannot put aside our anthropomorphic value systems of competition and power, of home dens and discrete, hard-won meals, of the giving of presents as a sign of friendship, all of which are the heritage of an animal that spends at least part of its time hunting, how can we expect a horse not to be hippomorphic? How can he understand that his very size seems threatening, his vegetarian teeth alarming? How is he, who relies on love, trust, and freedom to escape, to realize that we want him to tune into our desires despite the fact that we constrain and hurt him? Most of them lose that winged joyfulness pretty soon. Anything for a quiet life.

When I gave Rosie her freedom, which I am sure no one had done before, she said she wanted no more restraint; but she did not want to leave me. It made her realize that what had seemed like demands was actually advice. Ahead, the seeds of this possibility were being planted between Rick and Duchess as they journeyed over this openness with matching strides, putting their heads together to point out elk to each other. Their feet were golden with pollen. Duchess's worried eyes grew huge, and soft, and thoughtful.

The moon was waning, and under its brilliance the coyotes were running well, in full voice. In the night I woke to the sound of hooves. The horses, silhouetted against the stars, were skipping, wheeling, snorting, and rubbing their heads together. They were playing.

The juniper grew more frequent, thickening into little copses, and ponderosa pine started to appear as we traveled farther onto the plateau. Among the trees we found a small tank. Its sides leaped up at the sight of us as a blanket of frogs jumped in unison into its green waters, which flurried, boiled, and grew still. Despite the lush grass Duchess grew spooky, startling suddenly in the middle of eating as if there were lions about; when I climbed the side of the tank there were two young red bulls play-fighting not far away. They looked at me sheepishly and trotted away side by side.

At midday we come to Buckhorn.

There are places we reach in dreams and fantasies where tranquillity overcomes our restlessness, and all is peace, stillness, and light: nirvanas where there is no desire, no need for boundaries. Sometimes, when traveling, you come across them. If the ambitions of your schedule close the top of your head you think, "How pretty, must come back here sometime," and move on. But if you have no schedule, the sudden coincidence of inner vision and outer reality stops you in your tracks.

grama grass

In a golden glade stands a small pineboard ranch house. Ahead, the open landscape loses itself in scatterings of distant trees; behind, a ragged jumble of rocks rears up, covered in juniper with bark like alligator skin. Yucca and agave spike the crag. Bluebirds, those Navajo protectors of peace, swoop like dark violets over a scene that is not so much strikingly beautiful as humbly perfect.

The house was open, with a note to say that the owners, in abandoning it years before, would like others to enjoy and respect it. Rare visitors had left a book of appreciative comments. There was barely even a track to the house, which was so isolated that only those intrigued by the name on a map would find it; but they had treated it kindly, left a few cans of food, and swept the bare floorboards. The breeze sighed in the great ponderosa outside.

In a rickety shed we found a ton of dusty oats, which we sifted. In the paddock, grama grass raised its slanting combs of seeds, renowned throughout the West for their excellence as horse feed. On one side, from a gully choked with wild-flowers, a trickle of water ran over bare rock before plunging over a precipice into a chasm where the ground split open, revealing bare brown walls. A pool of brilliant green some sixty feet below marked the top of East Clear Creek, which winds roughly west to the Verde; its sides are so sheer as to render it invisible from the house, and impassable for tens of miles on end.

Dante wrote: *Nessun maggior dolore, che ricordarsi del tempo felice nella miseria.* "There is no greater woe than to remember a happy time when in misery." But the memory of a place of such tranquillity does not torment us in our troubles; rather, the knowledge that it continues to exist rekindles that nirvana, so that the "ten thousand things" are reduced to mere specks of dust dancing in light. The magical word "Buckhorn" produces in Rick and me such certainty of peace, harmony, and love that, whatever con-fusions our deluded ramblings may lead us into, its truth will always override them. I would wish everyone a Buckhorn glowing inside him.

At night, under a sky of luminous darkness, I sat on a warm rock among the crags. From a pool of shadow a rattle-snake spoke softly, lazily; when I replied in the same tone he saw no more cause for concern than I. Together we watched Rick in the paddock below, mazed among concentric circles of stones, stare at a sliver of a new moon.

We were brewing coffee under the ponderosa in the chill morning when a small posse of cowboys, dark with dust, rode through the paddock. We sprang to our feet, greeting them, ready with offers of coffee and explanations about oats; but they passed by only feet away without even glancing at us, as if we were in another dimension. Perhaps we were.

# chapter four

WHEN YOU WALK the maze, you seem to plunge into its problems straight away. But to your surprise it only gives you a foretaste of them before spinning you out onto the outer, more open circuits where progress is as free as flying. Unsuspecting, you swoop around a corner to find yourself caught, like a moth by lamplight, in ever-tightening coils.

We were not flying; we were sleep-walking, unaware.

Ponderosa, thickening, encroached on our dreaminess. Whether pine woods are generally depressive or whether I hate them from habit, for the planted blankets that smother the heartland of Wales, I do not know. There is no sky, no view, no sense of direction, no breeze to blow away flies. Finding dirt tracks, we made good time. But it was boring, and inevitably we came into areas that had been logged. The aftermath of felling, the splintered trunks, the squalor and violence wreaked by heavy machinery, made it look like a war zone. But instead of the familiar rosebay willow herb springing from the devastation, it was evening primrose, with its floppy yellow plates of petals, that rose breast-high for acres.

The unpleasant marks of humanity grew more frequent: fences, roads, clearings of paddocks and cattle. Later on, in a chill wind, we crouched on the slopes of a big tank in the middle of a flat dusty meadow, trying to make tea. A red motorbike puttered in our direction, two up. Apart from the ethereal cowboys, they were the first people we had seen for days. But they skirted us without stopping.

"Hi!" I shouted, making toward them. "Hello! Howdy!"

They kept on. Had our communion with nature rendered us part of the background? Their dark faces were set . . . their *dark* faces, framed with lank black hair . . .

"¡Hola! ¡Buenas tardes!"

They stopped immediately, breaking into delighted laughter and a soft singsong patter. Their Spanish was melodious and clear, catching the smiling intonation of the Indian rather than the machine-gun hammer of Madrid.

"Buenas tardes, señora. Have you seen our bulls? Young ones, red."

I told them of the bulls that had scared Duchess. "But they're more than a day away, beyond Buckhorn."

"We went to Buckhorn looking, but we went no farther. You were at Buckhorn."

"They went far."

"Oh, that's nothing. They can go for a week, down to Beaver Creek, if they want to."

Keeping track of your cattle over such vast spaces is a fairly hit-and-miss affair: "mavericks," the unbranded offspring of cattle that have not been caught for years, can outrun a good cow pony and are as nimble as goats. Bryce Canyon is a quite fantastic jumble of orange-gold spires and pinnacles that cover mile after mile of southwest Utah in a Gothic moonscape. When William Bryce discovered it, his first report was not an exclamation of wonder at the extravagance of nature, but the fruit of bitter experience: "Hell of a place to lose a cow."

It took us a day and a half to find the Willow Creek crossing. Like Clear Creek, Willow Creek is a 200-foot-deep, sheer-sided crack, and there is only one crossing in forty miles. By now we were in thick forest, and one of our problems was the Forest Service map. Each piece of lettering on the map was

not simply printed over topographical detail, but surrounded by a clear window so that it could be easily read. Willow Creek's little window apparently interrupted a track leading east-west across the creek: there, surely, was our crossing. However, forestry maps, including British ones, are frequently misleading, for in logged areas new tracks are driven, and old ones obliterated, almost daily; moreover, hunters proud of their all-terrain vehicles sometimes stab blindly into the forest, creating cul-de-sacs that others later follow. All in all, without any visibility it is impossible to tell which track you are on.

We checked out turning after turning. Sometimes we even arrived at the abyss, only to find ourselves at the top of a precipice staring at a tantalizing track that was an unreachable seventy yards away across the chasm. Duchess grew more and more jittery as branches plucked at her bags and rattled off the stiff canvas to bite her backside. Moving freely forward over open country, she could understand what was happening; here the endless backtracking and map-checking rewound the springs of her time bomb, driving Rick into a downward spiral of frustration and apprehension. In the desert, I had finally managed to withdraw from trying to alleviate his problems by retiring behind a barrier of enforced indifference, but Cedar Flat and Buckhorn had swept away the barriers, giving us space to fit into each other again. Now the dark forest, with its oppressive gloom, aerial rattlesnakes, and tortuous dead ends, set our nerves jangling until we were snarled up and snarling, able to agree only on the fact that we disagreed about everything, about attitudes to life in general.

We camped that night by a pool we had discovered the night before, in a little clearing alive with whirring grasshoppers. Deer tracks speckled the mud around the coffee-brown water. I kept fighting the feeling that we were inexorably sliding over the edge, being sucked into a black hole, and succeeded only in freezing like a rabbit.

"We can't go on," he said.

I laughed. "Magic carpet? Wish ourselves home?"

"It's not that," he said. "I mean us."

Over the edge. Nothing but the beating of my heart.

"It's not that I don't love you, admire you, want you as a friend. But as an entity we're no good. You think this is all right. I think it's a disaster."

I spent years making myself miserable, castigating myself for not being as good at organizing life as other people, before accepting my bumbling inadequacy and getting on with it. Ceasing to worry about social norms has brought rewards like having a mind free enough to notice psychedelic grasshoppers, but it makes me sloppy. To me this journey was a peripatetic part of life, so it was no surprise that equipment broke or we got lost.

Rick has much higher standards. To him, we were a farcical failure of an expedition. His underlying fear of Duchess was tantamount to being a sniveling coward in a world where I was apparently perfectly at home, and if this was my idea of home he did not want it. In fact, his control over his fear had me fooled; moreover, his determination to work his way through it meant he was unwilling to let me handle Duchess, with the result that I had little idea how scary she was. (Later, when I had more to do with her, I was aghast. "God, Rick, is she always like this?"

"She was a lot worse."

"Weren't you terrified?"

Downcast eyes, shuffling feet. "I thought I was just being silly."

"You would have been a damned sight sillier not to have been. If you can't recognize life-threatening situations, you really are a fool."

"I'm not a fool, I'm a coward."

"That's not cowardice, it's courage. Being brave isn't not realizing the danger, it's recognizing it and still going on. My hero." I don't know that I ever managed to convince him, but I sincerely admire him. When I am scared, I am quite pathetic.)

He meant it. My optimism only underlined our differences. Perfectionist as ever, he could not tolerate imperfections in our harmony, preferring to abandon the idea. Calm, serious, cold, he proposed that in a few days, when we were to reach a road and perhaps a telephone, he would walk one way and I could either appeal to Starr or continue with the horses on my own. It was not that he disliked me; but we did not belong together, he said.

Incompatibility. Apartness. Separation. Deeper into the heart of the maze, turning a corner to start another revolution, alone now, we wandered numbly through thorny thickets of self-deprecation.

It was bitterly cold that night. In the morning frost shimmered on the long grass, and the pool was thick with ice.

Silent and subdued, we tried again, pitting our best map-reading skills against the mocking forest. We were polite. It was horrible. Finally we acknowledged defeat. There was a ranch marked on the map, several miles away. Even that took some finding: it was in an area of "checkerboard," where alternate square miles are privately owned, often cleared, or belong to the National Forest. Of course, you have to be able to estimate a crow's mile on a wiggly track to work out which square you have reached.

It was a neat little pineboard bungalow in a clearing. The elderly rancher had the beautiful old-fashioned manners of the West. He admired Duchess, examined our cavalry saddles with interest, and admitted he used neither quarter horses nor western saddles. "I never rope cattle," he said. "You don't have to." He turned to his neighbor, visiting in a pickup.

"How many times you had to rope a cow?"

"Twice," said the old man, adjusting his battered hat with gnarled fingers.

"Twice in how long?" Rick asked. "A week? A roundup?"

"Twice in m'life."

It sounded like a mechanic confessing he never used a wrench. Massive sixty-pound saddles and horses built like steamrollers to take the strain of a roped cow are part of western dogma, so much so that our choice of horses and saddles had seemed to most to be a hallmark of ignorance. Roping obsesses rural youngsters and urban cowboys alike; riders who are adept with a rope call themselves cowboys even though they know nothing of the practicalities of keeping cattle. It was refreshing to find this thoughtful man discarding the dogma and extolling the virtues of hornless Australian stock saddles. He used Peruvian Paso horses, which do not walk, trot, and canter but scuttle smoothly at all speeds in a peculiar inherited gait. They are the purest descendants of the old Spanish amblers prized by medieval travelers like Chaucer's pilgrims.

He was not surprised we had failed to find the crossing. Its approach was not a track but a tiny cow trail obliterated by felled trees. We followed his detailed directions, picking our way over logs until the path turned into a slide of loose stones down a two-hundred-foot cliff. Hearts in mouths, we slid down, so steeply there was no possibility of stopping or turning back. If we were wrong we would shoot straight over a precipice. But we came to rest in an avalanche of stones in the creek bed. There wasn't even any water in the damned thing.

Getting up the other side was an equally uncontrolled upward slide, the horses plunging ahead of us unable to stop until, shaking and panting, we reached the top. At least drama concentrates the mind.

We came into rolling grassland dotted with big trees, like the parkland of a country estate. Chain-saw grasshoppers whizzed and clacked under the great oaks, and tiny blue flowers winked from the dry grass. Free of the forest at last, we settled into the gentle, pastoral rhythm of this new land. Though there were no signs of people, or tracks except cow trails, it seemed cozily domestic after where we had been.

A wild shriek rent the air. A skinny, desperate figure burst out of the trees, floundered down the slope opposite, arms and legs flailing, and tumbled head over heels to land beneath Rosie's surprised nose. He had a compound-bow, bowie knife, and army camouflage shirt and trousers.

"Where are we?" It made a change from "Have you seen my cattle?" But "Have you seen my elk?" was the next question.

It was the opening day of the bow-hunting season. Each year the Forest Service calculates the elk population, estimates the cull necessary, and allocates permits to hopeful hunters, specifying bull or cow quarry. Bow-hunters, who have a week for their kill, get first shot since their skill has to be considerably greater than that of a rifleman.

This young desperado had been woken at nine that morning by elk passing his tent. Grabbing his bow, he pursued them, lost both them and himself, and had been wandering for eight hours without socks, water, food, or seeing another human being. Smugly we handed him our water bottles and the last of our food, discovering he had come some sixteen miles southwest. He thought he had been going north. Remembering the heavy frosts at night, I wondered how long he would have survived, for he had no means of lighting a fire, and not a lot of sense. The likelihood of such loonies taking a potshot at Duchess, who was only slightly redder than an elk, seemed greater than that of finding a hunter who had not heard that the sun rises in the east.

The grass was growing thicker, but so were the trees, as we went on. Our next hunter was sitting in his chair, under an awning spread from a trailer, with his sitting-room, kitchen, and armory neatly arranged around him. A real camper. Rick gave me Duchess and went over to ask how far we were from Clint's Well, which would be our first supply point for a week. He came back and buried his head in Duchess's side without a word. Oh God, I thought, feeling the wafer-thin ice on which we had been tiptoeing shudder and threaten to tip us into inky depths. His shoulders were shaking.

"Rick?"

He raised his head, laughing helplessly. "It's hard to take directions seriously when the man's—" More giggles.

"*What?*"

"Green."

At Clint's Well, a café–filling station that we reached after dark, they were all green, though sweat had dribbled white stripes down their painted faces. Massive camouflaged bellies splaying over beknifed belts, they tapped grimy, or preferably bloody, fingers on tables as they waited for their fries. I had never seen Americans sit down dirty at the table before, but they did not want it to escape anyone's notice that they were Mighty Tough, these good ol' boys. To make sure, they bellowed it in bass chorus counterpointed by the treble quacking of their camouflaged wives. They were enjoying themselves hugely. I could not help thinking about the earlier hunters they had dispossessed for their swaggering charades, hunters whose red skin was not confined to the neck.

We ate a meal, from plates, sitting at a table, before setting off half a mile down the tarmac road. Headlights blinded us. Behind me, Duchess's footfalls suddenly stopped, then started again with a wild clatter.

"Rick?"

"She just leaped ten foot into the air."

"Not much farther. Hang in there."

Turning into the black forest, we could see more hunters' camps, spotlights glimmering through the trees, emanating an uproar that surely sent any self-respecting elk miles away; but we got directions to what we wanted: government horse pens, stoutly built, and a grama-grass paddock.

At 7500 feet in a damp pine forest it is achingly cold at night; and well before dawn the hunters started crashing about, making unearthly wails that are supposed to sound like elk calling. The elk's bellow starts low, jumps an octave suddenly, and tails upward into a screech. A lousy approximation is made by dragging a tight-fitting wooden piston through a tube, but elk are apparently so randy they will go for that. Or so I'm told. There were far more hunters than elk: the beasts were all safely on Cedar Flat. But the din woke us from too few hours of shivering sleep.

I peered out of the tent at the old timber corrals. The short grass was white with frost; above it rose blackened stalks of locoweed. Duchess was carefully avoiding it, but she looked gaunt, ragged with exhaustion. Worried horses will not lie down to sleep, and although they can doze standing up they

only sleep soundly, and dream, when they lie down. I had
expected them both to lose weight for a while before packing
it on again as muscle; Rosie looked harder and fitter, but
Duchess looked fit only for a rest cure. We were heading into
higher, wilder country unless we begged Starr to bail us out.
Our brief contact with civilization seemed to have restored
Rick's sense of adventure, but I could not count on him. I
reached for the map to check the prospects, but found none.
We had lost it.

Fire-smoked tea on a bitter morning is delicious but does
little real good; it is the sun, when it at last clears the trees,
that warms your bones and blood, breathes hope and courage
into you, and sets your clothes steaming. Once you look and
listen with hope, the rewards flood in. We went back to the
café, where the waitress rang her boyfriend to bring us a map
from twenty miles away; we phoned Starr, who was incredu-
lous at our progress and said she could come out in a few days
with more supplies; we found a ranch where a lady related to
the man with the Peruvian Pasos sold us masses of oats and
told us of a fenced area near a lake a day's ride away; and on
returning to the pens we met a man who became a good
friend. Nick was a real estate agent from Phoenix, who
spent a few months a year profiteering in the smog in order
to keep himself camping up here for the remainder. His
easygoing philosophy, humor, and warmth found instant
sympathy with Rick.

"So you've come over Cedar Flat," he said, as we squatted
around a fire brewing coffee. "Sure is beautiful up there. I was
up there one time in the fall, after the rains. It gets real
treacherous: the water lies in the draws, so they turn to
swamps. As you know, there's nobody up there, least of all at
that time. All of a sudden I see this vehicle coming over a
rise, having a real hard time, what with all the rocks and
marsh. Then I see it's not one but two: old bull-nose Dodge
trucks loaded with mattresses and stuff, *The Grapes of Wrath*
fifty years on. They were tied together with a bit of rope.
Every time the front one got stuck the back one'd ram him

from behind and bump him out; every time the back one got bogged the front one'd haul away. They were two guys from Arkansas, going to California. They hadn't a lot of money for gas so they'd worked out the shortest way without bothering about whether there was any road or not. Sure beats the hell out of going Greyhound."

We had to go on after that.

Potato Lake was perfect: a long green meadow ringed by trees and a sagging fence we mended in cold moonlight. By the lake the pale bark of aspen glowed. Unlike other trees, aspen belong to the night. They are moon trees, ghost trees, ethereal and mysterious in their ceaseless whispering. The horses drank the dark waters calmly, raising their heads to gaze around, holding the last mouthful of water between pursed lips so that it dripped softly, then dipping to sup again. They sighed happily and said it was a good place.

We decided to stay and rest for a few days, exploring the area. Our southward trail had led us gradually higher, and we were almost on the edge of the plateau, where it stops abruptly at the Mogollon Rim.

At my grandparents' farm was a barn with stone steps leading up to what had been the laborers' loft. My grandmother, a massive dynamo, loved country-house sales, from which she would often return with piles of books. The "upstairs outside room" was a repository of the discards and duplicates, ton upon ton of them, deep enough to burrow into on rainy days when you could not take to the woods or fields.

I was what was called, frequently and with exasperation, a "difficult" child. Unlike my sister I had no intuitive grasp of socially acceptable behavior, and far too much raw passion. Despite the variety of our extensive family I was perpetually out of step with everyone I knew, though I tried so hard I would end in furies of frustration and hurt. There was no such trouble with the animals, the excitable dogs, the pigs with their cheerful, optimistic charm, the moony, angst-ridden cows, the irritable old racehorse, or my cynical pony.

I could talk to them or the tame jackdaws, predict the movements of badgers, or befriend toads and owls more easily than commune with my family.

The books to which I fled were slyly subversive, showing me other modes of life, other social mores, places where I would slide as easily as a hand into an old glove. There were places where to want to spread one's bed under the stars, drink water from a stream, and sit by a fire listening to night animals following their secret lives would not be greeted by cries of "Don't be so ridiculous!" and immediate incarceration in a square-walled cell.

It was there, among the half-comprehended treasures, that at the age of eight I saw Edward Curtis's photographs of Navajo filing past the cliffs of Chelly and knew immediately that the vague feeling of not being my parents' child, of being a misfit, was true. I was an Indian. I started sleeping on the floor and trying to make pots with the red clay of the deep-cut streams. My secret friend, whom my sister had jeered out of existence, reappeared, this time wisely unconfessed, as an Indian mentor. What he told me about how his people lived, what they believed in and how they related to their world was uncontaminated by television, films, or comics: it came surging up from the longing at the back of my mind and turned out, as I came across a few facts about real Native Americans, to be almost unnervingly accurate. Gray Owl, with his wonderful little drawings of beaver lodges and moccasin-making, lived too far north for dream scenarios; it was Zane Grey's *Young Lion Hunters* that, despite its arch-cowboy attitude of defeating the wilderness, provided a perfect setting. The Mogollon Rim, where Grey lived and wrote, had for so long been one of my secret places that it was hard to believe we were perched only a couple of miles away.

We rode on a pilgrimage to Baker Butte. At 8200 feet it is the highest point on the Rim. From the top of the fire-watcher's tower, above the trees, you can see half of Arizona: north, across the dark rolling forests of the Coconino plateau falling gently from the Rim's uplifted edge, to the faded

yellow and pink of the high deserts; west to the San Francisco Peaks, the sacred mountains of the Navajo and Hopi,
where the kachina spirits live. Only a few yards to the south
was the Rim itself, a massive two-thousand-foot cliff running
east-west for a hundred and fifty miles. Below, beyond the
wilderness of the Tonto Basin and over the blue Mazatzal
Mountains, the golden Sonora Desert was darkened by the
revolting haze of Phoenix and, over a hundred miles to the
south, the faint smudge of Tucson. But even their sprawling
self-importance was dwarfed by the vast panorama of smoke-
blue peaks rising perkily from mysterious forests or umber
mirages.

Such a scale, even when you are there, is difficult to grasp:
imagine standing in the middle of England and seeing sea on
three sides, with half of Scotland on the fourth. It is not
merely lack of elevation that is the limiting factor, but the
haze of humidity and pollution. To be able to see so much
land at once is baffling. You cannot comprehend, only be
amazed. "I've been here eight years and I'm only beginning
to understand it," said the fire-spotter, a trim, elderly lady.
"Folks think I'd get lonely, but often I put up my NO ENTRY
chain across the ladder and pretend I'm not here, to avoid
company." In winter, when snow blankets the high plateau,
she and her husband camped in a trailer down by Lake
Roosevelt. She seemed utterly content.

We descended the ladder and were once more in thick
forest, with no sense of the abyss that yawned only yards
away.

Horses have remarkable memories for places they have
been. On the five-mile return to Potato Lake, Rick let Duchess pick her own way through the multiple-choice paths in
the forest. Except for once, she unerringly took the right
path, even showing us a couple of shortcuts. But it was
memory, rather than direction, that guided her: the map
showed that there was an altogether shorter route. Finding
herself undirected, her equine talents accepted, was odd but
pleasing to her: she became concentrated and confident,

rejecting little Rosie's attempts to make helpful suggestions and snarling at her when she tried to overtake.

In the chill of early morning, Potato Lake steamed gently and the dawn sun caught the tops of the aspen in a blaze of gold. There were prints of elk and deer, badger, and the long, delicate hands of raccoon in the mud. I once slept in a hammock in the Florida woods for two months, and used often to wake with those little black hands brushing softly over me, or toying with my hair, while the clown-ringed eyes surveyed me thoughtfully. People warned me they were dangerous. It took me some time to realize how urban most Americans are, and how likely to regard wild animals as enemies. *Le tigre, c'est un animal très méchant: quand on l'attaque, il se défend.*

Starr is a genius at presents anyway, but in dreaming up a feast for us and the horses she excelled herself. Grapes, peaches, melon, cheeses, smoked salmon, steak, salad . . . We ate and drank and laughed for hours, joined by Nick, who had tracked us on his bike with an armful of clothes, thinking we might be underequipped for the cold of the Rim.

"I can't believe it," Starr kept saying. "Doggone it, *Jim* can't believe it. Something's got to be looking after you, you've been so lucky." But I did not feel *lucky*, except in her generosity and friendship: it seemed to me that we were treating the earth right, that our respect and love allowed us to wander unscathed, as if having so few demands won us the right to have those few granted.

Though we try to make sense of things, I do not believe there is any. I cannot believe in any god except the unifying force of life itself, whose ramifications are so miraculous as to fill a lifetime with wonder. To watch an amoeba crawling, or a spermatozoon fertilizing an ovum, under a microscope is to see life naked. The emotional impact of that life force, stripped to its barest essentials, devoid of any purpose greater than that of maintaining itself, yet instantly recognizable as that which drives you too, is shattering. *I am that I am:* no more.

Most animals see no problem about this. They live without, as far as we can tell, worrying about the meaning of life. But our evolution involved a rapid hypertrophy of the part of the brain that deals with logic, with cause and effect, and gave us a powerful analytical tool: language. The two are inextricably intertwined. It is impossible to conceive a complex rational argument without language although, to our constant frustration, language and emotion are not so bound up. Finding the right words to express our emotions directly is notoriously difficult and unsatisfactory: we find it easier to deal with them at one remove, in myth and allusion, or nonlinguistically, as in music. Expecting our emotions to behave logically is equally unsatisfactory: often the best we can do is to collect painful evidence as to the patterns of their behavior.

This mind-body dualism (assuming you follow the ancient tradition of placing emotions where they feel as if they are, in your heart and guts) has its basis in neuroanatomical fact. Reason and the "brute emotions" are dealt with in different parts of the brain. Our brains are much bigger than most animals', but they are selectively bigger: the parts that deal with appetite, or hormones, or emotion for that matter, are no bigger than they are in a horse. It is the massive overgrowth of rationality and language that gives our brains their extra size.

It also gives us a massive selective advantage, particularly in a land where climatic conditions are liable to change so rapidly and drastically that several wholly different lifestyles may have to be adopted within one lifetime. The ability not only to observe connections (which animals can do) but also to analyze, hypothesize, test hypotheses, and record the conclusions even when the conditions are no longer present is human, so much so that it occupies most of the play of tiny children, and many of our communications as adults.

But this ability, which we prize so much, leads us to some ld conclusions, such as the assumption that every effect has a cause. Logically, then, there must be a Cause for the biggest effect of all. You can call it God in any of its numerous names, only to find that teams of bureaucrats have gotten there before you, had meetings to decide what should be the party line, and muddled it with morality and social control. *Theology is the enemy of religion.* In any case you have to accept that Its (His, Her) logic is impenetrable, which seems to defeat the object of the exercise. You can believe your destiny is written in the stars, or in the ceaseless interplay of Yin and Yang, or in how you have behaved in previous lives. You can, like the Hopi, believe that if you do not treat the things that give you life—sun, water, corn—with reverence, then things fall apart. However you look at it, that powerful neocortex will be analyzing, reasoning, trying to fit it into some watertight pattern.

We lay around the fire, as people have done since they first discovered how to control it, watching the flames and discussing the meaning of life, as people always have done, and this meeting of travelers in warmth and companionship seemed a timeless instant, running like a thread through the millennia. Starr's offerings of strips of charred and bloody meat, Rick's sooty fingers feeding the fire, Nick's cross-legged musing, these were the universal gestures of humanity itself in its element. I am that I am. Above the flames flying sparks raced with shooting stars.

"Look!" the little bird was saying. He was a smart navy blue fellow, darker than the usual bluebirds. "Look: big seeds, here, and here, and here." He picked them up and dropped them, to show her, then stood with his head cocked quizzically. But his wife was not impressed.

"I don't know what you think you're playing at, you stupid fool. *Look out,* will you!"

"But it's quite safe. Look, it's lovely, all bare: you can hop around quite safely. Do come down."

"I don't know what you take me for, dragging me all this way . . ."

He had been visiting us for three days, cleaning up the oats after the horses. That morning he brought his drab, nagging wife. We heard him when he was a way off, having a hard time persuading her gradually nearer until he could display his new-found-land while she perched, grumbling and shrieking unnecessary warnings, on a branch overhanging the clearing. He was so proud of his discovery, standing on tiptoe to demonstrate its excellence, and she such an ungrateful shrew. When she did fly down it was only to shrug off his achievement disdainfully. You don't need words, or even thoughts, to have quite complex emotional reactions: it tends to take a lot of words to describe the exact shade of meaning behind a wink or a shrug.

It was in this peaceful meadow, where plentiful food, water, and salt were beginning to replace the flesh on her gaunt frame, and daily baths in the lake were refreshing her, that Duchess started at last to acknowledge not merely that we would not hurt her, for even she had realized that by now, but that we might be worth considering as companions. When a new horse is introduced into a group, the others usually reject it for three or four weeks before including it in their social bonds. Rural communities do the same, though they keep it up for longer. There is no point in wasting emotional investment on possible fly-by-nights. We had been together for several weeks in all, and the pattern of our journey was becoming obvious. Time was eroding her resistance. We would catch her staring thoughtfully at us, not because we were dangerous, or for tidbits that she always refused, but because we interested her. She would stroll into camp, touch the tops of our heads as we sat cooking, smell us again and again, and rest beside us. It is quite possible that she had never really examined a person to her satisfaction before. We tend to be so busy doing things with horses, or brushing away their attentions lest they hurt our precious skins, that we do not let them accept us voluntarily, in their own slow time.

Rosie, of course, was a different matter. She rooted through all our gear, singed her whiskers in the fire, and scared herself picking up plastic bags while we rested for the next leg of our journey: the Mogollon Rim.

 chapter five

GENERAL GEORGE CROOK was sent to Arizona in 1871 to subdue the Apache and confine them on reservations. Between his base at Fort Apache, just south of the eastern end of the Rim, and Fort Whipple, near Prescott, he established a supply trail, most of which runs along the very edge of the Rim. Now a Historic Trail waymarked for hikers and riders, it had been enthusiastically recommended to us as one of Arizona's great tourist experiences. We followed it eastward for two days before admitting the unthinkable. We found it boring. O heresy of heresies! It is equivalent to saying that the Grand Canyon is a boring hole in the ground.

But it *was* dull: dreary, depressing, monotonous. You simply followed a swept path through ponderosa monoculture for mile after mile. The magnificent view was hidden behind fifty-foot pines except at select viewing points, carefully signposted bits of bare rock at the ends of promontories. You cannot do much with that kind of view except stare at it for a while and go away. There was no way to absorb it. We could not camp anywhere we could see it, nor even brew up a cup of tea, for there was nothing for the horses to eat. Even staring could not be done peacefully, for other viewers drove up along the Rim road, which crisscrosses the trail, to declaim loudly about how wunnerful it was and drop cans. One was a hard-faced, vulgar woman who traded with the Navajo and Hopi to stock her gift shop. She sneered as she spoke of them: they were a lazy,

thieving lot who asked too much for their goods. I wondered
what her markup was. She said we would not be welcomed on
the reservations, nor be allowed to camp. Momentarily dis-
heartened, I revived my spirits by reflecting that if I had a
reservation I would not welcome her either.

We passed through two big burns. The Baker Butte fire-
watcher had told us that the Rim burns were notoriously
difficult to fight, for the updraft from the cliff fanned the
flames and made helicopter spraying highly dangerous. In
the first was a sign that read:

WHAT HAPPENED HERE?

An abandoned campfire, which was discovered on June
4th, 1990, in the Tonto National Forest, caused the
destruction you see before you. The Bray fire scorched
633 acres (259 acres below the Mogollon Rim on the
Tonto National Forest and 374 acres above the Rim on
the Coconino National Forest).

On June 7th, 1990, this disaster was finally brought
under control. It took 696 people from 10 agencies to
accomplish this. The final cost to the taxpayer was well
over $1,500,000.

Remember, only you can prevent forest fires.

For as far as the eye could see, blackened stumps rose from
garishly brilliant green grass in a haunted, inverted parody of
a forest. Dante might have used it next to the suicides' wood
as the repository of souls whose pleasure-seeking led to mass
destruction. Yet there were still scores of fire-rings left by
picnickers. Each had to make his own fireplace, apparently:
when you're Conquering the Wilderness it does not count to
use a ready-made one, even if you drive to the spot with an
icebox of supermarket stores.

Only a few miles on was the infamous Dude Burn, a
thousand acres of it. Local prisoners are sent to help regular
firefighters, just as Faulkner's prisoner was sent to work on
the Mississippi levees in the great flood. These amateur

firemen are issued heat-reflecting sheets to erect as canopies, under which it is possible to trap enough oxygen to stay alive while the fire sweeps overhead. It sounds like a terrifying act of faith. Perhaps because their nerve failed, six prisoners had not used theirs properly, and were incinerated. This fire also engulfed Zane Grey's cabin, perched below the cliffs.

Our *Guide to the Crook Trail* directed us to a meadow clearing near where Crook had massacred a bunch of Apache, a Historic Event because it was this slaughter of their defenseless women and children that led the Apache to accept life on a reservation. There was also a Historic Cabin, carefully labeled, built in 1919, and some seeping water that was supposed to be a spring. But there was no fence. Before we left we had taught the horses to tether—that is, graze on a thirty-foot rope without getting tangled up. Feeling a rope snaking round his heels, a naïve horse will lash out, catching the rope in the hollow of his back heel and, by sawing against it with his heel, burn himself horribly; but by a series of approximations he can be taught to watch and avoid the rope. Rosie had learned well, but Duchess's neuroses included a phobia of ropes, one cause of which was the old rope-burn scar on one back heel. I had abandoned her lessons, thinking that she would not stray if we tethered Rose; but she had shown that she would be only too happy to leave us. We had no option but to tie her somehow, yet she had to be able to graze. Given her panics, the other option, hobbling—that is, tying the front legs together to restrict her movement—seemed inadvisable.

We tried picketing her in a gully knee-deep in rich grass, tying her with a running noose to a high line strung between two trees so that she could stroll up and down like a dog on a clothesline; but the gully spooked her. It was justifiable: no wild horse would get itself caught in a gully for fear of lions leaping off the side. There was nothing for it but to try tethering again. Despite furious protests about her scarred heel I managed to bandage both back ankles. The whole affair took hours and hours.

In the middle of the night I was up and running before I was awake, frosted grass under my bare feet, calling to the struggling fallen horse. No burns, but she had contrived to catch the rope between her hoof and the back of her shoe, and her kicking had wedged it in. I danced about trying to extricate it as she lashed out, but finally had to cut it. Rick was disgusted.

"It's completely crazy to be out in the middle of nowhere with this mad horse. Asking for trouble. This isn't an expedition, it's a farce."

"It's neither, it's just a part of life, and life's full of problems," I repeated wearily. "We'll solve them. She's getting better, you know that. This is just a temporary setback, don't worry."

He sleeps more soundly than I (oh bliss, to have a peaceful sleeper in your bed. I was married for years to a man who never stopped twitching and kicking) so he did not notice how many times I got up to check her. But I must have slept for at least two minutes, during which she burned herself, though only slightly.

Ponderous ponderosa. Trail without challenges. I imagined the jingle of cavalry, far more isolated than we, trotting through the woods in terror of Apache; and the wagon trains that followed, the creaking wood, the mules staggering and slipping over the rocks, the whiplashes and shouts; but it did not amuse me for long. Thunder rolled along the Rim. It rained, which amused Rick at least.

Our next water was at Lost Lake. We could not find it. Rick says I blamed him. I probably did. For hours we went up and down the same half-mile of identical burned trees, scientifically quartering the whole area, the horses getting as irritable as we were as they fell over old tree stumps. We must have passed within yards of it twenty times, for it was exactly where we had thought it should be. It was a marshy pond; but to our joy there were aspen, and fresh grass in the burn, and enough trees to picket Duchess.

In a pale, cold dawn the long marsh-grass was gold around the steaming water, and a huge bull elk gleamed bronze under the aspen. Duchess neighed to him and he ran away. The air was freezing on my face. Rick's warmth as he slept, the smell of him, which has a hot line straight to my emotions (more neuroanatomy: it does, unlike the other senses, which get the rational analysis), made me want to cry out and burrow under his clothes; but we were out of step, I wide-awake and cold, he warm and dreaming, and he would not have appreciated it.

I lit a fire and made tea, watching the light change, wondering what the hell we were doing. A hundred yards away, invisible as ever, lay that immense vista; but we were in the forest, each overshadowed by our private frustrations, wounding ourselves on the broken branches of our dreams. Lost at Lost Lake. When Duchess spooked at the ghosts of her past maltreatments she only hurt herself again; but we were no better. Both Rick and I subject ourselves to the torments of the damned, the black holes that suck you into a nothingness from which there is apparently no escape. When you realize that you create them yourself you only appear doubly doomed.

Feeling unutterably silly, I watched the weak sunlight fade as thunderclouds built up from the south. Rick dragged himself out to join me, moving in slow motion.

"We seem to have got ourselves in a bad place," we intoned drearily. He knocked the pan of tea into the fire, putting it out, then filled his boots with mud wading out to reach more slime-free green water. I fell over searching for more wood, spiking myself trying to reach the only tiny clumps of dry needles in this sodden forest. We both know better than to fight this stuff; you just have to endure, and try not to poke yourself in the eye with your dirtiest finger. It began to rain. It didn't even have the decency to do a *Lear* tempest, despite the thunder. Duchess, whom we had parked on a guaranteed snag-free picket, managed with great ingenuity to walk around and around the anchor tree at one end until her rope was so short she could only stare balefully at the bark.

"Why do you do it to yourself?" he asked her sadly. "You don't have to be there."

Some people see horses as workthings, some as playthings. Some tend them like herbaceous borders, others use them to achieve ambition, or status, or relaxation. Miserable adolescents find they can confide in them, megalomaniacs find they can dominate them, nervous people find them nervous. They are mirrors. They reflect us faithfully, warts and all.

"Why don't we be somewhere else?" we said simultaneously, banging our heads together as we retrieved Rick's damply smoldering boots from the fire.

We abandoned the wunnerful Crook Trail, which we had been intending to follow east for two or three more trouble-free days, and turned north.

The high Coconino plateau rises to the Rim itself. Rain falling on the edge does not plummet over the cliff but collects in puddles and ponds, the outflow running north, away from the precipices, carving out a series of ever-deepening parallel canyons. It is an unusual arrangement that anyone with experience of the way land works finds difficult to accept. We found ourselves on a ponderosa-lined dirt road that ran along the top of a ridge between two canyons. Tourists' cars whizzed past, choking us with smelly dust.

"I barely like to say so, but this is another kind of awful," I said.

"At least it's easy," Rick said. "At least we'll get there."

"Get where? I don't want to get there, I want to be there. Here. Now. Look, we've got food, there's water in these canyons, there's no advantage in being on the road." And I wheeled Rosie and plunged off the top of the ridge down the side of a wide canyon.

Two hundred feet below, it was beautiful. Huge oaks stood in russet clearings fringed with bracken. There were birds—ponderosa, of course, has no little birds—which fluttered and twittered. Squirrels busied themselves among golden leaves. Deer wandered away, browsing. It was like hearing Mozart after acid rock.

We sat stunned for a long while, drinking in the rich soft shades.

"So?"

One glance at the map showed that it was impossible to take the jumble of canyons seriously. But there was a lake several miles to the northeast. There was also a campsite, which we neither wanted nor needed, but which might have some supplies. Starr had said she would come out once more, to a lake where the fishing was said to be good, but none of us was certain when we might get there.

"We'll follow the Way," I said. There was no trail; there was no view; there was no wind, nor sun to direct us. Sometimes, though, it is better not to think and direct, but to let intuition take you where it will. The yellow sky was raining, but in the woods we were dry as we drifted along talking of Laotzu. The soft light gilded the turning leaves with the hues of autumn, for this was deciduous wood—hickory, ash, and oak interspersed with the ivory-sheened aspen—and bright with butterflies and birdsong. We followed deer trails from clearing to clearing; every now and then an internal compass nudged me gently. It was easy.

Rick quite suddenly underwent a change of perspective, a rearrangement of perceptions. It was here that he said, slowly and wonderingly, "I see that I have been a cowboy, where you're an Indian." In that day he let go of his anxieties, his self-doubts about whether we were doing this thing properly or not, or whether indeed his anxieties were a symptom of his failure, and all of the complex towering edifice he had built on top of his head to weigh him down. He understood that we are made for this earth, and if only we let our senses guide us properly, then all will be well, however far we may be from the safety nets of civilization. It is not difficult to understand intellectually, but quite another thing to feel that you can trust it and live by it miles from anywhere. It is not an attitude that our lives normally permit: however much we duck the rat race, cars still have to be licensed, bills have to be paid, appointments to be kept, and these imperatives crush the subtleties of our more delicate intuitions. Rick has always been able to give time to them within a Confucian structure of duty, but throwing that framework away altogether and finding that everything did not collapse was a revelation. One of his most admirable qualities is his ability to apprehend, without rancor, wholly different points of view; as I saw his face and body change, easing into an unworried pleasure in our situation, a carefree confidence in our abilities to cope with it, I was overwhelmed by joy and love. Deer watched us peacefully as we glowed our way through leafy glades and aspen dells. Presently, with as little effort as if we had been floating downstream, we found ourselves at the edge of a campsite.

The rain was sheeting down, but as soon as we had located the best patch of grass for the horses' midday break it stopped abruptly. Rick went to borrow water from a family in a camper-trailer, and returned with a shovelful of fire and two unbelievable cupcakes for our tea. Dripping with thick dark chocolate, they were soft, rich, and succulent. O lady, unlikely as you are to read this, let me heap praises as thick and rich on the excellence of your baking and your goodness of heart. Never can two cupcakes have been more appreciated.

Beyond the campsite clearing there was a cattle grid over the track leading to the lake, and a large sign saying NO HORSES. We were not about to lose, though: slithering through the trees we found a bit we could undo with our trusty but unused fencing tool (hitherto, its only function had been in balancing the saddlebags, for it was the easiest thing to swap from side to side), redid it superbly, shot down to a pine-lined lake screaming with speedboats, bounced over the retaining dam at the end, and dissolved in the woods within minutes and without being spotted.

We wandered on through the gentle woods, dappled now with sunlight. There were no signs of humanity among the fallen leaves, nor undergrowth to impede our passage. Trackless beneath the thick, fleecy canopy we had seen from Baker Butte, the forest floor rolled in ever-increasing swells as we padded past badgers' dens and wild bees' nests, its constant murmuring rustle broken only by the shriek of blue jays or the rapping of woodpeckers. In the evening, at just the right time, we naturally reached another of paradise's doors, a broad meadow whose green grass glowed in the slanting light. Aspen lined the slopes on each side, their leaves tinged with gold like the bracken below them. A real spring bubbled clear and cool from the moist springy grass. There was another Historic Cabin, this one built as far back as 1911, before they had invented windows. Duchess seemed quite content to stay around for once, trailing an untied length of rope, until we were visited by elk up at the far end of the meadow. She showed a distressing tendency to go charging after them, neighing shrilly: she was in season, the silly bat, and blind as a hunter.

Directions feature strongly in most Indian philosophies. The details, and the principal colors or animals used to symbolize them, vary, but the general idea of the directions of the Medicine Wheel of life is so universal as to be reflected in the Greek idea of the four elements, in Pavlovian conditioning experiments, and in Jungian analysis of character types.

In the east, direction of the sun's rising, is the cold, clear light of first dawn, the most dispassionate and objective illumination of our lives. It may be yellow or white, though to the Apache, Sun is often black, and the Hopi sometimes see it as the deep purple that precedes the dawn itself. It is the far-seeing vision of the eagle soaring above the plain of everyday life; scientific detachment; pure intellect; it is sitting on a Welsh mountaintop seeing where the tidal waves of humanity, from pre-Celt through Roman to Victorian slatemen, reached before falling back, and understanding that your troubles amount to nothing.

In the south, the heat of the day, is the vividness of emotion, the innocent exuberance of life and fertility; trust, laughter, warmth. The Green Man belongs here, with Dionysus, and parrots, and little short-sighted mice that feel with their whiskers; and probably Mick Jagger, too. It is lying with your lover and not giving a damn about anything else, and it is the bright green of life itself, or rich turquoise, or even scarlet.

In the west, where the sun goes to rest with his woman the earth, is introspection, self-analysis, the black bear. The revelations that come from within as you sit wrapped in the shaggy pelt of your own thoughts belong here: meditation, protective self-knowledge.

In the north is the night, where intuition guides and the wisdom of the buffalo, the mysterious influence of the moon, direct us as they directed me through the trackless woods. Night holds no terrors for those who have MacNeice's "white light in the back of my mind to guide me," and it is often associated with white.

None of these ways of experiencing the world is more valid than any other; they form points of view like those of a circle of watchers around a campfire. But each of us emerges on a certain point in this wheel to make our journey through life, over the great plains of possibility with their healing waters and clever coyotes, the slow-moving turtles of tradition and obsessive dragonflies, plaiting our braids of experience as we wander first one way, then another. There is a time and place to follow each direction: the purpose of the journey is to travel the whole circle, as the world itself does. We cannot live in eternal night, nor eternal midday, without becoming static and unbalanced. It strikes me that often in our Western world we are encouraged to do just that. When a child shows a talent in a particular direction we try to keep him on that path, to the detriment of his exploration of others. But the pressure to compete and excel has no place in the formation of a whole human being.

Rick had been traveling on a spiritual East-West axis; now he wanted to try North-South. His guidance led us through country so rich, varied, and hilarious that it seems impossible that all my mind's pictures belong to the same day. Geographically, the main canyons run back roughly northeast from the Rim; their side-branches, then, run east-northeast or north to join them. We needed to go a bit south of east to our meeting place with Starr, so all the country was against easy progress, though definitely in favor of exposing its surreal spectrum of creativity. We made five miles in a hard eight-hour ride.

Hillsides of bracken, a solid blaze of brilliant gold, a color that even we Welsh connoisseurs of bracken had never dreamed before; scarlet-leaved maple rising above it, so spindly-trunked that only the fluttering red rags could be seen; little clumps of rich green juniper in regular triangles; magnificent spreading oaks overhanging ravines; all these were strangely reminiscent of our own country's games, and held the same elusive sense of small snoring dragons curled under rocks, or unicorns not-quite-visible to our unvirgin eyes. It was sheer magic, made even more so by its dream-like quasi-reality, for familiar trees such as ash, rowan, or holly were not quite right, the pattern of leaves or bark recognizable yet transformed, like American English. In one of these Celtic canyons a tiny face peered from leaf mold: the owl face of unfaithful Blodeuwedd, the woman that Gwydion the enchanter, a trickster if ever there was one, made from the flowers of oak, broom, and meadowsweet to be Llew Llaw Gyffes's wife. I leapt off with a cry. It was half a black walnut.

And then we would cross the crest of a ridge and plunge into another, quite different world. Great blue spruce, majestic and sacred, whose needles were yellow nearest the bark, then green, tipped with deep smoky-blue, lined steep-walled canyons where sweeps of green-gold grass formed enticing motorways leading the wrong way. Another canyon would be emerald-black pine, or lime-green larch. Dropping into these canyons through tight-packed trees, we slid down elk trails winding around crags and rocky outcrops, narrowly avoiding shooting straight over them. Elk are smaller, narrower, and nimbler than horses carrying packs, but the horses were by now firmly convinced that any trail was better than none, and seemed to have lost all concept of their size. We found ourselves blocked by fallen trees that the elk hopped nimbly over, or in tunnels through thick brush, or on paths so steep that we could not stop but had somehow to continue madly, falling and slithering, until we all met again at the top or bottom to gaze in wonder.

Rick took out the map to inscribe in his beautiful calligraphy: *You can only be lost if you are trying to find something.* We, of course, were not at all lost; nor were we having any difficulties in sliding backward through broken lances of pine toward precipices, or picking our way through quaking bogs in the canyon floors. We did not have to try, or find: we were there. The valleys with their shadows of death held neither evil nor threat but a vast, all-embracing harmony: the tinkling of water, the deep bass of the spruce, the soft sighing of the pines, and above it the wild, triumphant bugling of the elk.

We finally came to rest in a blue-spruce canyon. Hail was falling. However hard it rains you can crawl into a blue spruce and stay dry. The elegant cone, some eighty feet high, of downward-sweeping branches sheds water like a duck's feathers. The lowest branches start about eight feet from the ground, which they dip down to touch before turning up again. Inside is a tepee, not big enough to stretch out in, but bone-dry and utterly peaceful. A spruce breathes serenely, and you are inside its breathing. When I crawled inside one for kindling, all the other trees being dank and dripping, fleeced with wet moss, the shock of this intimacy almost made me flounder out again, as if I had interrupted some intensely private scene, or had found myself inadvertently raping it; but I fought back my embarrassment and let go, allowing the tree to breathe me. It was some time before I looked down to see the perfect twigs it had graciously laid at my feet. No wonder Hopi recognize spruce as sacred.

The sun has to rise high before it begins to penetrate one of these canyons, "so steep they have to bring the sunshine in in wheelbarrows." Without any "they" or wheelbarrows, I lay and shivered. The tall grass was gray with dew. The light crept slowly down the smoke-blue slope opposite, glinting off wet crags. When it reached the bottom it spotlit a family of wild turkey, Hopi symbols of the wilderness, foraging at the edge of the trees. The eastern part of my mind does not know what to make of these northern truths, this feeling of blessed gifts.

A mock-elk bugled from the top of the ridge above us. To my horror, Rick bugled back far more accurately. I rugger-tackled him into the trees. Bleary-eyed hunters are far more dangerous than any wilderness. But it meant there had to be a trail up there.

We emerged from another steep climb onto this trail, and found a dirt road a few miles later. Almost immediately Nick rode by on his little bike.

"Why, hi, how're you doing?"

We brewed tea and told him of our adventures.

"If you want something hard enough, it happens," he said. This was going a bit far for me, even with my conviction that most things are moved by faith and determination: Starr's "meant to be" or "not meant to be" is pure tautology.

"If you don't get it, it's because you don't want it accurately enough," he said. "Most people don't know exactly what they want. It's a question of being able to visualize it in every detail. I had a friend who taught me that. One time we were hiking, and we came to a river. It was real hot, and we'd come a good ways, so we sat on this riverbank just longing for a cold Budweiser. 'Okay,' he said, 'all you got to do is think of it. Visualize it. Believe me, it'll work.' So we thought so hard our brains nearly burst. We could see the lettering, the way it wrapped around the cans, the exact shade of red, and the drops of condensation frosting the cans as they sat in front of us. All of a sudden a four-pack of Coors came floating down the river. Well, we fished them out and I said, 'I guess it does work, but the only thing that puzzles me is that we asked for two cold Buds, not four warm Coors.'

"'It ain't finished yet,' he said, and just then a pickup drives up beside us. Guy gets out, goes to the icebox in the back, and brings out a can of cold Bud.

"'Say friend,' says my partner, 'you wouldn't care to swap

a four-pack of warm Coors for two cold Buds, would you?'

"'Sure,' he says. 'Here you go.'"

We moved down the road to our meeting place with Starr, a picnic spot above Bear Lake reservoir. We had chosen it because she would be able to find it and would be able to fish, and we would be able to graze the horses and maybe bum food off visitors if she did not turn up. There were no visitors, and the bare ground under the pines was innocent of grass. Nick was interesting Rick in a plan to hunt hunters for food, since they always came oversupplied; but in the afternoon Starr turned up, with a whooping cohort of friends, trucksful of food and beer, and yapping Chihuahuas. Their loudness and high spirits were bewildering after the gentleness of the woods and Nick's soft voice: Nick belonged in the woods, anyway.

I moved Duchess away from the party, to a good clearing some fifty yards away. She had become pretty reliable on the tether rope, and if by chance she did get it around her legs she had learned to stand still for us to free her. We settled down to make pigs of ourselves. Rick seemed to be doing fine, but I could not join in the merriment. I felt utterly alien from these people. One of them, who had been a pretty girl, was in some biochemically altered state, and her ravaged face, uncoordinated limbs, and frantic, jerky speech, which appeared to seem unremarkable, amusing even, to everyone else, filled me with unexpected anger and horror mingled with confusion about being prudish. I drank more beer. It did not help.

Starr had bad news. She had been on a fishing trip with her father when he started to feel faint. By the time they reached the hospital his pulse was twenty-five. "Guess this is it, Starr." But they had fitted him with a pacemaker, and as she said, with more than an echo of him in her voice, "Now his heart'll beat away at sixty a minute come hell or high water, whatever happens to the rest of him."

It was difficult to know what to say. He is a man who would hate infirmity.

Suddenly a white camper-van shot into Duchess's clearing and screeched to a halt in a whirlwind of dust. The door flew open, releasing a blast of music and a California swinger with an enormous frizz of yellow hair and skintight pink shorts. An ear-splitting screech of appreciation of the wilderness scared Duchess into bolting for safety toward us. But the rope was against her, and by the time I reached her she was down, enmeshed, struggling.

I led her back. She limped. The rope had torn all the skin off her left back ankle, the one we could not handle. Sickened, I gave her a pile of oats.

"You know," Starr said thoughtfully, "that horse ain't got fifty miles left in her. In fact, I'd say she ain't got twenty-five in her. In *fact*, I'd say she's finished."

I had been feeling better about Duchess. Her weight loss, inevitable when an unfit horse takes to traveling, seemed to have halted. I had felt she was picking up, putting on muscle, since we had hit the cool high country. But now, as I looked at her with Starr's eyes, I saw a miserable, shivering, exhausted bag of bones. She was pitiful. Rick looked almost as bad. They would both give themselves hell about her injury. (In retrospect, I can see that I did not make allowance for the way that horses, like people, seem to shrink when they are in shock: my own shock, and the drink, the feeling of alienation from Starr, the thin ice between Rick and me, and our situation—for we could not now ask Starr to bail us out, with her father ill—were not conducive to sensible diagnosis.)

"We'll find some good grass by the lake," I said slowly. "We'll rest for a couple of days, and stuff them on the oats you've brought. It can't be more than five days to Winslow after that, and then we'll see. I don't think we can ride to Hopi anyway: there's barely a blade of grass in Navajoland, or water, and there's the Little Painted Desert to cross. We'd have to leave them in Winslow and hitch."

But it felt like doom, even among the gaiety. Rick withdrew into serious drinking. Trying to keep a grip, I searched through the maps Starr had brought, for we had reached the edge of ours, but none was the right one.

In the evening, when they had gone, I went down to Bear Lake. Steep pine woods ran straight to the water's edge, leaving a stony shore. The rampart of the dam was bare, too. Precipitous paths made by fishermen led down the rocky slope to the lakeside. Any horse, let alone a cripple, would risk its legs there. But below the dam was, as I had hoped, a gully where rich grass glowed in the last of the light. Satisfied, I went back to check every step of the way, moving a boulder here, a fallen tree there, until I was sure that with care they could make it. I fed them again, and arranged a picket. Duchess refused to let me even look at her ankle, and Rick was dead to the world. I seemed to spend the whole night shivering, in an endless fall, waiting to hit the bottom.

Hangovers never help. It took us hours to pack up, loading everything on Rosie and ourselves, for we had practically a full sack of oats. Making Duchess take the first steps was agony: rope-burns ooze fluid, which then sets and cracks again and again. We crawled down to the parking lot at the head of the path. Rick looked horrified.

"I'll just check again," I said. "Don't worry, it looks worse than it is."

When I came back, everything was scattered all over the place, Rosie was unladen, and Rick was smoking peacefully.

"What happened?"

"She took off. It was the oats, I think. Wasn't anything I could do. She just bucked it all off and came back. Well, at least I'm learning not to jump after them when it's hopeless." He seemed quite cheerful.

We descended the winding path down the crumbly cliff, step by painful step. Feeling horribly guilty, I kept promising it would be all right once we reached the dam. Rick groaned at Duchess's every wince. Finally we stood on the dam. The horses gazed at the lake in astonishment: our previous lakes had been no more than ponds, but this was huge, deep blue, and sparkling in the breeze. They put their heads together to consider.

"There!" I said triumphantly, and ran down the rampart of the dam to my lush grass.

I sank right up to my thighs. It was a marsh.

We arranged a poor picket on the sloping rampart. The grass was meager and dry. We made a fire, and coffee, and had a blazing, horrible row. What kind of horsewoman did I think I was, he wanted to know, dragging that pathetic beast down a precipice into a marsh, after wounding her through my own bad judgment? He was right about the last bit: he had said she would be too far away, but I had overridden him. It stung. If I hadn't practically had to carry him all the way, I said, I might have half a mind left to think with. It got worse. I threw my coffee over him. He finished his calmly, poured himself another cup calmly, and poured it over me.

I took Duchess, whose leg was so swollen that I suspected she had sprained a ligament, and stood in the lake with her. Crawdaddies nibbled my toes. The voices of my childhood mocked me: *You are hopeless, Lucy.* The sense of having been born wrong caught up with me again. I'd been fooling myself, as usual, mistaking a gap in the clouds for some kind of certificate of heavenly approval. And to end the farce, what had come out of the middle of me was vicious, intentionally so, unforgivably so, to the one person whose deep honesty had not only rescued but sustained me, and whose gentle sensitivity could least withstand it. All he had done was finally to acknowledge the unwitting destruction I carried within me, which his love for me had denied to the point where it no longer seemed to exist, even as a figment of my imagination. But his perspicacity in recognizing, in this relatively trivial incident, the tip of an iceberg of possibilities was enough to make him turn away self-protectively, enough to reignite my rage against myself and vent it on him, enough to plunge me into the icy depths of total recall.

I have tried to get away without the next part, but all the

meaning disappears, leaving only a narrative of a not-so-remarkable journey. If you're content with that, don't read the next chapter. I wish I did not have to write it, or that I could express what is of value without having to be so autobiographical; but we had reached the center of the maze and there was nothing but raw truth.

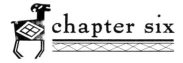 chapter six

THESE ARE THE BARE bones of it. Quite a skeleton. I try to refuse to give it closet space, but equally it refuses to die entirely, leaping out from a look, a glance, a phrase.

It was not until my fourth miscarriage that I really began to doubt the doctors who shoved their hands up me, patted my knee, and said there was nothing wrong, keep trying, next please. I stopped trying to have any, but they kept coming anyway. Two or three later, advances in technology enabled a determined surgeon to discover that I had a partially divided uterus. By that time I was divorced.

You can sit down and talk to yourself until you accept the inevitability of childlessness with cool rationality; but persuading a fertile body to relinquish its inner drive is another matter. Mine was devious, refusing to tolerate reliable methods of prevention and making me inept with others. It was not difficult to clock up a couple more losses, nor to deal with them: early ones are not bad, especially when you have trained yourself not to hope.

Years later I met a man . . . Oh, I was wrong, I was culpable, but learning to deal with culpability without the attendant guilt that makes you squirm, feel ashamed, run away, make excuses and misrepresentations, that was the hardest. It was only when we were heavily involved that he revealed that by "I've left my wife," he had meant, "emotionally, not physically, you understand." I should have got out then, but I did not. It was not as if anything were being destroyed: his marriage had become total war, without the Geneva Convention. But I muddled that with a disregard for truth. You cannot build a healthy structure on shifting sands; but I came in for ceaseless vindictive bombardment, too, and in steeling myself to rise above that, I also disregarded the subtler but more destructive flaw.

To me, on the other hand, he behaved well after he left her, until, a year later, I became pregnant again. He left me while camping on a hillside in Spain, shouting, "How do I know it's mine?" I moved on fast, lest he find me.

I knew I would lose it, of course. I worked part time on an avocado farm, living in a tent almost wholly on oranges and avocados, licked my wounds, and waited for the inevitable. I was quite calm. It was a time of great peace and beauty, the hillsides sweet with lavender and rosemary. I shared bread and garlic with two old men, learning the Andalusian dialect, stroking the inside of the avocado canopies to find the heavy, swollen fruit.

Time passed, and it did not happen. The later a miscarriage, the more serious. I did not want to end up in a Spanish hospital, but I could not afford the airfare home. When I said I would hitch to Madrid for the bus, they turned the hens out of a wonderful old jalopy, a twenty-five-year-old *Deux Chevaux*, and spent two days dragging it up and down with the tractor until, with triumphant shouts of "¡Arriba!" it purred into action.

"I can't accept a car," I said.

"It's not a car, it's a henhouse," they said. "It won't go far. When it dies, just bury it."

Oh, *la belle* Titine! Her name was painted on the steering column amid a shower of hearts. There were no seats: the driver's seat was an avocado crate. The windshield wipers were manual, worked by a knob you turned furiously until your arm ached. The headlight dip, too, was manual: you turned another knob, which turned two rods going sideways, which turned two rods running forward, whereupon the headlights, slowly, gravely, bowed their heads until you winched them up again. The handbrake worked, but was so loose you had to jam it fast with a sardine can. She jumped out of first unless you forced the gear lever in place. The roof was a torn, faded American flag. But she went *anywhere*, all day on a bottleful of cheap petrol, even if it took an octopus to drive her.

We went more or less straight across Spain, Arkansas-style, without benefit of roads, for I suspected that the flimsy scrap of paper they dug out did not constitute legality. We took mule tracks, cart tracks, sides of fields or hills in our stride, which was a brisk walking pace. Once I camped in an enormous olive grove that covered several hillsides. I had just boiled my tea in the dark when headlights came over the hill. Hastily I doused the fire and hid behind a tree away from the car, which was hidden, too. The headlights drew nearer. Torches. Voices. They found the car, and called.

"Why doesn't he come out?" they wondered, starting to swear. They discussed this curious behavior. One of them had an inspiration. "Could he perhaps be a woman?"

"A woman! She would be afraid."

"Don't fear, *señora,*" they called. "We are honest men, doing our job."

At that, I had to come out. They invited me to spend the night with them. I said thank you, but no, thank you. They were, they said, the guardians of this land. "And we will guard you, too. No one in the bar will know you were here, until tomorrow when you are gone. It is not safe for a woman alone."

"That's what I was afraid of," I said.

"Ah, but we are honest men. The others, now . . ."

They woke me in the morning. They had already made a fire, and coffee. There was a spotless white napkin laid on the ground, with bread, cheese, and *chorizo.*

In a week we were in the Pyrenees with the eagles and the skiers. Driving through farmyards we were greeted by dogs like fleecy white bears that poked their heads through the rents in the flag to slobber on my hair. I cannot recall how I talked my way through French customs. It was the smallest frontier post, and Titine had French plates, but it took hours even so. I telephoned my insurance company in Porthmadog: maybe the sound of Welsh convinced them I was so *complètement folle* that they were better off without me.

A week later, only thirty miles from the ferry, the police caught up with me. I had followed pig tracks through the chestnut woods of Périgord, driven through miles of vineyards and sampled their wares, shivered in the dank plains of the battlefields. They could not believe I had got that far without being stopped, for I had no *carte verte* (green insurance card) on the window. I said I had seen no police, but they could not believe it of France. And my documents were *complètement inutiles*, a farce. They added up my fines: over £250. I stuffed my £30 ferry fare in my bra and held out my 15 francs.

"I have no more."

"But you must have."

"I haven't. Here, look in my wallet."

"Then we cannot let you pass. *Il faut*, you understand, you *must* pay now."

Impasse. "In that case," I said, "all I can do is give you the car. It must be worth something, it's antique." Reading his label, I filled his name in on the useless form, gave it to him, took my rucksack, and started to walk across Normandy in the dark. He ran after me.

"You cannot abandon your car there, it's forbidden."

"It's not my car, *m'sieur*, it's yours."

I had gone perhaps a mile before they drove after me, siren wailing.

"We will send Interpol to Penrhyndeudraeth, *madame*. Meanwhile, go, *with your car*."

I drove to a café, opened a magazine, and found myself looking at a butter advertisement showing a cow on a field the exact shade of green of a *carte verte*. I cut a square the right size, inscribed it with my insurance information, drove past hordes of police onto the ferry and home to Wales. It snowed all the way. My wrists hurt, but I was still pregnant.

Two weeks later, four months gone, I started to bleed one night. I phoned the doctor and got the wrong one on duty. He told me not to worry. I said, "I'm old, I've had nine miscarriages, I'm half a mile from a road up a steep mountain, alone, and forty miles from the hospital."

"Take an aspirin and phone in the morning," he said, and rang off.

I was on my own, in a small open boat, in the middle of a stormy Atlantic night, and land had voted itself out of existence. Trembling, I waited for the big one. And waited.

What came instead was a call from the local schoolmistress, to whom I poured out my troubles, which no one else knew. That afternoon the district nurse arrived, panting from the steep climb, a woman whose sense and friendliness seemed, despite the spotlessness of her uniform, to bring the comfort and warmth of a farmyard: the tradition of hundreds of years of care that infuse those solid-walled barns thick with straw, where generations of animals have safely struggled into life. The sense of haven in her touch almost made me break down.

She sent me to the hospital.

They did a scan, pointed out arms and legs. It did not change anything. Yes, at present there was this growing inside me, yes, it was called "my baby," but there had been others, too, and I had studied my embryology, I knew what it would look like and what was going on. They did an amniocentesis, plunging a huge needle into my belly, because I was old and because I did not want a Down's syndrome child on my own. I would make the same decision again. As the needle went in I was overwhelmed by terrible panic, but told myself not to be silly. Of course it would look alarming; yes, it did slightly increase the chances of miscarriage, but they were almost certainties anyway. Afterward, they did another scan. He was thrashing about as if in a tantrum.

"No, no," I cried, "they've hurt him."

"It's all right," the nurse said, laughing. And I fought to remember that he was not much different from a stickleback whose pond has been stirred. Even amoebae retract from things as if they were mortally offended.

They gave me a room of my own, for which I was thankful. The heat of the ward, the terrible semiconsciousness that many pregnant women happily drift into, would have made me rude. I joined them for the wholly unsuitable meals they ate with relish: chips, pies, chips, jam roly-poly. A gypsy woman used to come in for secret smokes. "Gawd, Luce, you're the only one alive in 'ere." We sang an old music-hall song beloved of my grandfather, who danced to it while feeding the hens:

> Treat my daughter kindly, say you'll do no
>   harm,
> And when I die, I'll leave to you my little
>   stock and farm.
> My horse, my cow, my ox, my plough, my
>   cottage and my barn—
> And all the little chickens in the garden.

Exhausted interns came in for a nap, curling up at my feet like dogs: "Wake me in ten minutes, don't forget."

I bled very slightly, on and off. It was, they said, a low placenta: nothing to worry about unless I suddenly went into labor, in which case things would have to happen fast. It could be any time, which was why I was there. But I could go for a walk every day. The fields were full of lambs and oxeye daisies.

Pregnancy, even when you refuse to allow yourself to imagine its consequences, profoundly alters the way you think. It is no longer a question of how you can understand the world, but of how the world relates to your child. Politics, ecology, the state of the world, all become personally involving in a way that they did not before. How are you to bring up a child in a world where people behave as they do? Greed, heartlessness, or any other of the wrongs that we perpetuate, become not merely irritations or disappointments but threats to your child. How are you to teach him to love, and trust, and be open, when people do such terrible things? Even now when I look at the photos of those starving babies in war-torn countries, I look at the eyes of my child.

I tried to do things right for him, but I did not let myself dream (which was why Nick's conviction about the cold Buds struck a note of horror). "When this is all over you'll find it was worth it," the nurses would say. "I've got to get there first," I'd reply, but honestly, not grimly. It crept on, day by day.

My friends, and even people who live in the same valley but whom I do not know so well, made the long trip to bring me their goodwill. The whole valley seemed to put its arms around me. The schoolmistress came and talked for hours about the children she had taught. She remembered every one. Brought up in a tiny rural Welsh community, she left home for the first time to do her teaching practice in Liverpool and Manchester. Shocked by the squalid rawness of poor urban life, she remembered, forty years on, the name of every child, which one's father was a drunkard or beat him, which one had no father or several, who brought what for lunch, and her efforts to comfort them. When she left she apologized for talking about herself, but it was the best of presents, knowing that others would cherish him, too.

I went for walks, and began to write a bread-and-butter book that my publisher, with great kindness as well as his usual astuteness, had suggested. And waited. They treated me not as a late miscarrier, but as a pregnant woman. They weighed me, and listened to his heart. The conceptual leap from the blood and pain of a miscarriage to a—what? chubby charmer? destructive toddler? pimply adolescent? was baffling.

I had to get to twenty-eight weeks before I could dare to hope, for at seven months, a baby, though very premature, is decently viable. But we all knew that at any moment my uterus might decide it had had enough. To our surprise, it did

not. He was very lively inside me: I could feel every movement, feel him asleep, or stretching, or rollicking about.
Simon, a friend from the valley who had moved nearby,
brought me music. As time passed I realized how much he
could hear, down there inside me. Rock 'n' roll had him
rocking and rolling, the frantic disco beat made him twist
about unpleasantly, but Mozart held him absolutely still, yet
alert, as if he were concentrating.

At twenty-eight weeks they sent me to Liverpool, for they
said he was bound to be early, and we would get the best care
there. My daily strolls took me down streets of boarded-up
shops, fish-and-chip shops, or barricaded shops selling liquor
or ripped-off car radios. It seemed a city at war. But there
were art galleries, Stubbs's Molly-Long-Legs with her wicked
eye, and Augustus John's perceptive portraits of Liverpool
aldermen, and squares of rose gardens to lie in, and a kestrel
nesting in the roof of the warehouse opposite my room. And
we were safe, he and I, safer as day succeeded day.

However, I seemed to be wetting myself slightly. It had
happened all the time I was in the hospital, but it was getting
worse. They said it was quite common: stress incontinence,
caused by pressure on the bladder. But I had excellent control over my bladder, I protested. They tested my dribbles, for
I wondered if it was the waters leaking, but their little test-
stick said not. But it bothered me.

Twenty-nine weeks. Thirty weeks. I began, very cautiously,
to hope. I had made no plans; I had nothing for him. But he
would have to stay in the premature unit for some time
anyway. I knew I would manage when the time came. Meanwhile, I let myself enjoy him being there in my strange huge
belly, listening with me, letting me learn him. The only
thing missing was his father's seal of goodwill. I knew he had
tried a reconciliation with his wife, and though I could not
believe it would work, I had no wish to disturb him. But I did
wish he would at least send us some small message, overcome
the guilt that doubtless hounded him and compounded itself,
just one small sign; but guilt is a demon master.

The miracle went on. Blessed, *bendigedig*. Ben. Miracle. Impossible reality, kicking away vigorously.

One night I crept from my bed, raided the supply cupboard for one of their little sticks, and tested myself. It was as I had thought. I was losing amniotic fluid.

I told them the next day, but I started labor too. Thirty-one weeks. I could barely believe it. I welcomed each great roll of my belly, a paean of triumph raging through me, stronger as the day went on. They would not let me drink: there had never been any question but that I would have a caesarean. The rolls got wilder, closer, a storm. Dawn was breaking when they said: "We'll take you down now."

I welcomed the needle like a friend, babbling nonsense until their laughter faded into darkness.

Being wheeled around. Doors. Curtains.

"Is he all right?"

"Just a minute, dear."

"Is he all right?" But she'd gone.

"Is he all right?"

"Wait a moment, dear."

"Is he all right?"

"She's to go there. Give me a hand."

But I knew.

He was absolutely calm, the poor man they chose, handsome as an angel, careful, and infinitely kind. He spoke slowly, trying to find out how conscious I was. I said: "I come around very fast, lots of practice. He's not all right, is he?"

"We can't be certain yet, but I'm afraid he may not be. Let me try to explain. Late in development, a baby's lungs gain elasticity by breathing amniotic fluid, what's called the waters, in and out. If there is not enough fluid, the tissues of the lung do not develop that elasticity, and the lungs cannot expand fully after birth. Do you understand?"

"Yes. I was losing my waters, so he couldn't breathe."

"Not well enough. We are—" *are:* He's alive. "—giving him oxygen. It may be that in the next few hours his lungs will respond better, and that he may—" *may, may, may* "—pull through."

"But you don't think so."

"It's too early to tell. How well do you feel?"

"Fine. I could get there."

"Not without a wheelchair."

He was tiny. Not wizened, just tiny. Beautiful. Strong, from all that activity. Round-limbed. He lay on a pad with tubes coming out of him, oxygen going in. I stared. His limbs moved in rhythms I knew from inside me. The heat was unbelievable. The morphine froze time, froze me. I watched, willing each movement of his chest. He was so strong but so fragile, so miraculous.

"You can hold him if you'd like," the nurse said. I wanted him to have the best chance. Perhaps I was wrong, but I felt it would disturb him, increase the demand on those flagging lungs. I shook my head, stroking him instead.

"We can take the tubes out, if they disturb you," she said. I was furious. "No, it's not that—"

As soon as he heard my voice, he rolled his head over and looked at me. And in that one look, wide-eyed, slightly puzzled, everything in me, my whole body, my soul, my will to live, *everything* went out to him. I had not thought . . . Of course, all those months, my voice . . .

Hours later, I was still stroking him, in that dazed incomprehension that morphine brings, when a man came in. It was Dave, a Liverpudlian friend of Simon's, a lighthouseman from Bardsey Island. Ynys Enlli, island of the saints, otherworld of cold air and sea, gull cries, clarity, peace . . . I realized I was falling, falling . . . a blinding headache . . .

"Dave, it seems awful to leave him, but I've got to go out for a while."

He wheeled me around in cool corridors, found cups of tea. It was a day and a half since I'd drunk anything, in that heat.

"It's a bad show, Dave."

His hand on my shoulder. Gentle man, gentleman. Confused and embarrassed maybe, speechless maybe; but rising to this impossible situation, a friend of a friend, in the depths of unknown womanhood they find themselves most incapable of dealing with capably. Good as gold.

Revived, we went back. He was even smaller, his gray eyes huger, but he moved less.

"What do they say?" I asked.

"He's putting up a good fight."

I stroked him. A few hours, the doctor had said. But many hours had gone, and he was still there. I thought of Enlli, of a child running on the cliffs. My child. My son. But I was confused too, muddled by wishes and heat and exhaustion and morphine. My head didn't work, only my heart, willing him.

They said: "Do you want to hold him?"

"I can, but don't take the tubes out; please, please don't hinder him."

I slid my hands carefully under him, and held his small weight, and I knew it was no good. Growing up on a farm, you nurse many newborn things: pigs, calves, lambs, puppies. You know when they're not going to make it, and when there's even the faintest of hopes. I tried, my head tried, my heart tried, everything in that look tried, but my hands told me.

As the hours passed he lost his rosy flush, growing limper and grayer.

We were back in my room, talking of Enlli and laughing at a story of Dave's girlfriend, when a head popped around the door and said he'd gone. We went straight back to the conversation for a minute. Effectively he'd gone when I left an hour earlier: he'd been comatose, blue. Should I feel I abandoned him? He wasn't there.

When a ewe has a stillborn lamb, she looks around at it, sniffs, nuzzles a bit, loses interest, shakes herself, and goes off to graze. When a ewe has a live lamb, her nuzzling provokes movement, which stimulates more nuzzling and licking. It is called bonding. If the lamb is sickly and dies, she will stand for two days in the field bawling over the spot. Even when the body is removed she will come back to bawl.

Bawling. Bawling. The whole body howling, right down to the roots, the roots that make life possible at all, the link that must be forged if life is to go on, the raw end of the severed link gushing out passionate incomprehension. Basics. A gap in an arch, bridged with one look, a slender keystone, and shattered again. Bawling. No, basics. Setting the thing in motion is trivial in comparison, an act that may be graced by love and beauty but that works perfectly well without. Mere mechanics will do for procreation. But for what is procreated only love will do, especially when times are harsh, to rise above the doubts and fear, the pain and the problems, for survival.

(It's easier this way. How else am I to write it?)

And that look, that touch, that tiny key to the totality of acceptance must, absolutely must, complete the link if the helpless life is to survive. That transference from self-protection to baby-protection, from self-interest to baby-interest, must be switched on fully, instantaneously, from the first moment. If anything, it must be strongest at first, waning as the baby develops his own self-protection. Most women, of course, ease themselves into it more gradually, with months of dreaming, knitting, and talking. I had not. The impact was not one of shattered dreams. It was of the blind fury of nature itself, raw, savage, elemental, cheated out of a destiny for which she had quietly been preparing unwitting me. Maenad furies howling, bawling, bawling.

The cries of babies being taken past the door made me want to batter myself against the walls. Milk would pour out of me. There was no escape. I could not even run away and gallop furiously over mountainsides. They said it would be a fortnight before I could leave. But every moment was an infinity, a maelstrom of torment. Printed words meant nothing. Music was all his, empty without his echoing dances within me. There was no time: when people spoke, each past word dropped into nothingness, so that I lived in an eternal present.

His surprise, to find himself evicted from his merry pond into a world that slowly crushed him to death, its only recognizable feature my voice.

Dave, who lived nearby, called Simon, who came. First, though, he sent word to the father, who called and said he could not come. Would not come. How guilt makes cowards! How cowardice makes people guilty!

Simon was extraordinary. Sympathy and kindness we can all give to our friends in distress; but tact, the ability to know exactly what can be done and when, is a real gift. Skillfully, patiently, with infinite delicacy, he succeeded in creating moments when I did at least function, however stupidly.

After three days I was walking to the bathroom, furious at the doubled-over, self-pitying shuffles of my fellow cae-sareanees, when I met a woman I'd talked to in the prenatal ward. She had had two stillbirths, and had been awaiting her third baby with the same reservation as I.

"What happened?" I asked.

"I had a little girl," she said, almost shamefaced, for she knew the savage, jealous anger. But for her I had none. Almost to my surprise I felt happiness sweep over me, the first pleasure I had had since the needle went in. Suddenly I knew exactly what would stop the pain.

"Will you bring her to me?"

"Do you think that's a good idea?"

"I know it is. Don't you see, she's the only baby I could face."

She let me hold her for hours, anxious but knowing that being in such a state does not follow the logic that others suppose; and my body, its wild hunger satisfied at last by the only thing it wanted, found peace. Living in a succession of eternal moments has its compensations if even one of them is right. The baby slept calmly on my chest. Finally the mother became worried that she would never get her baby back.

Dave, Simon, and the nurses hatched a plot. Dave's flat, behind the hospital, was in a block that many of the nurses lived in. A neighbor had gone away, asking Dave to tend his plants. Could I finish my fortnight there, in a kind of ward annex?

Being relieved from the constant presence of baby cries was some improvement. There was an outside world. Behind the flats lay Toxteth, boarded and shuttered, for the most part abandoned. Packs of dogs trotted jauntily through streets littered with brickbats, waist-high in golden ragwort, marking their gang territory on the wheel-less wrecks of burnt-out cars.

Dave's friends, penniless on the dole but exuberantly creative, succeeded in interrupting my weeping. But it was as if my grief resented interruption, for every moment of relief was followed by redoubled pain: I had no right to forget, even for an instant, that puzzled look of recognition. This was to be the pattern for months to come, as was the sense of living in the interminable present. Platitudes about time healing are meaningless when there is no time. For months I could not remember in the afternoon what I had done in the morning. I would forget, between one hour and the next, to whom I had spoken, and of what. The blackness that descended obliterated everything before. Ragged with exhaustion, I felt sick all the time. Simon once gave me a dinner plate on which was one pea, a slice of carrot, and a tiny sliver of meat, saying he had at last figured out my idea of a meal.

I went home at last. The support of my friends surrounded me with love and kindness. I believe that it is this, rather than the mere passage of time, that accumulates to heal us. Where faith and hope fail, charity, that greatest of human attributes, still sustains.

We buried him in a corner of the graveyard on the hill, facing the mountains he would have frolicked in. The preacher, a friend, said: "In his small lifetime he created so much love." Would that all our lives were so blessed. Every spring, unrequited, a solid clump of oxeye daisies springs up there. How was he so powerful a focus?

Despite my friends, it was terribly lonely, all that emptiness. It sucked me into the black hole of the damned. As the immediate shock wore off and I became capable of thought,

I was left not only with a self-replenishing well of grief that forcibly expressed itself at regular intervals, but also a feeling of inherent badness: not deliberate wickedness, but innate destructiveness. In all innocence, I had caused his death. I had wanted an amniocentesis. They had warned me of the risks of miscarriage, but did not mention the far smaller, indeed practically negligible, chance that what did happen, might. It would have made no difference to my decision anyway. But what I did killed him. The difference between "it was because of what I did" and "it was my fault" proved, in the talks with friends that everybody said would help, to be imperceptible to anyone else, and in trying to explain it I would get so upset I upset them. They cried out that I must not blame myself or feel guilty, that I had done everything I could, it was just bad luck. It was precisely that that made me feel damned. Whatever I did, with all the good feelings, intelligence, thoughtfulness, and love that I could muster, I only created loss, destruction, death. The difficulty of explaining that this was not a matter of mere semantics, nor of having made a mistake from which there might be something to be learned, alienated me from them. My talking about it, even quite composedly, distressed them. As I came to realize that they could not perceive the distinction, I saw that it was my inherent badness, and their innocent goodness, that made me able to comprehend things they could not, and that association with me would contaminate them so that it would be precisely their innocence that would lead to their downfall and destruction. I was a kind of walking embodiment of the Black Death. Closeness to me had brought death to everything I had cared for, my parents, the many friends I had lost either through death or parting, even my old stallion. I was a being whose very nature could not help but destroy others, and, it being the essence of me, could not be overcome by my own efforts and will. Even he, that miracle entrusted to me, had been consumed by it.

The conviction grew stronger and stronger until there was no brushing it away, or thinking that it was temporary megalomania, the egocentricity of the deeply unhappy. There was no escaping the conclusion that I should kill myself. But this logical conclusion simply pointed up some deep illogicality in the argument, for more death, destruction, grief, and guilt (I do not think I flatter myself: I have seen the effects of suicide on those close enough to feel they could have affected the outcome) were exactly what I was trying to avoid.

There was no guilt attached. I had long ago realized, through watching the antics of people who indulge in it, that guilt never helped anything. You can make reparation, learn from mistakes, vow never to make the same again, but merely feeling guilty inevitably leads to worse outrages, evasions of the necessary work. Perhaps it was because I had programmed guilt out of my possible behavioral repertoire of responses that I drove it deeper inward, and thought myself as damned as Oedipus, though by whom or what I could not say.

When I forced myself to stop toying with the elements of this network and, instead of trying to push them aside, think through the ramifications, I saw, as you no doubt have already done, that there was something severely wrong in the state of Denmark.

I took myself to a counselor who, having lost a baby herself, was in a position to know what contortions we get into when we try to make sense of things for which there is no sense. After several meetings she asked me to write down all these destructions, losses, and rejections. I added all the relationships that had ended, for I regarded them as being wise moves on the part of those who realized how dangerous it was to be near me. The list took a week and covered pages: a painful exercise. When I read it over I was aghast. How was it possible that I had not killed myself before? Where does my zest for life come from?

I started to write again: all the feeling, the joy, the love, the goodness of friends, the kindness and sustenance of those who believed in me . . .

I rang her up. "You swine," I said. "You manipulative, scheming fiend. You knew what would happen, didn't you?"

She laughed delightedly.

But there was no such exercise to remove the pure grief. Talking about him merely made me able to talk about him without embarrassing people by bursting into tears. Social practice. The awfulness of his struggle remained.

I went back to Liverpool for a checkup. The doctor said gently: "Look, physically you're in good shape, and I won't be seeing you again. It may be a little premature to be saying this, but don't let this blight the rest of your life. Many women do. I know they feel that to put it behind them would somehow dismiss the validity of the baby's life; but I beg you to go forward, when you are ready."

And I have done; but why is it impossible to write of it, six years later, without it seeming as if it were yesterday?

Months later my son's father reappeared and enfolded me in his arms. Oh, the foolishness that weakness lets us in for! Loneliness makes us grab at straws. But he wanted me; he also wanted, now that he had truly extricated himself from the vengeful marital war without any interference from me, to behave as a decent peaceful citizen. I met his little daughter, and the look in her shy, puzzled eyes released all that pent-up maternal feeling, scaring me into sensible caution. But I could not help loving her as my own, taking it as a personal triumph when the lifelong bed-wetting stopped almost immediately, watching her flourish and grow strong and rosy, learning to gallop over the hills shouting with joy. Her laughter was sunshine, her increasing confidence a tonic.

The mysterious persecutions continued, the obscene telephone calls, the strange behavior of my car. It was hard to tell what was paranoia and what was real. But I could afford to feel arrogantly above it, for I was needed, and I was proving that steadfast kindness was as valuable to others as it had been to me. It was only by clinging to this belief that I withstood it, for malice, be it provoked or unprovoked, takes its toll.

One day I answered a knock on the door to find two burly

men in macintoshes, with the local copper hovering around them.

"I'm sure there must be some mistake," he began, but they brushed him aside.

"CID," they said, holding out a search warrant. "We have been informed that you are concealing the baby that was stolen from Cardiff last week." They were looking straight at the bottle I was using to feed a pet lamb.

I beat the wall until my fist bled.

A year passed, but there were increasing difficulties, compounded by his ever-increasing drinking. Forgetfulness, evasion, truth sliding under layers of excuses, the lovely numbing jollity of drink leading to more unconfessable situations, the defensive attack of shame . . . I did not want to recognize the depths of moral decrepitude into which we had both slithered. I was just as bad; I lied to myself, unwilling to face the truth: that the tenacity of my belief in the power of my honest good feeling had led me into a wholly dishonest situation.

One night he did not come back. Such was the loyalty of his drinking cronies that it took me a couple of days to find he had gone off with a woman down the road and was having a riotous good time.

For months the little girl and I were trapped, unwilling witnesses to their affair, like rabbits mesmerized by a stoat. He did not return. We went to Portugal on a horse-buying expedition for a friend. She stood in the crashing Atlantic, daring herself to brave the breakers and succeeding triumphantly.

One day she did not come back from school. He had taken her, without telling me. Wild with grief and rage, as any mother would have been, I found him two days later. He tried to run away from me. I grabbed his shirt. It tore. "You're mad," he said. "Get away from me, and don't come near her again. She's my daughter, and she'll do as I say."

It was as if I had lost a second child, but this time the grief of loss was compounded by anger of a degree I hope I shall never experience again. He was well-practiced at evoking it: if you can provoke the woman into excessive behavior you can say she's mad, which justifies you. It practically cost me my sanity not to kill him; but I would not allow myself the luxury of revenge, which I had so much despised, and I felt a fool, too. In a small community you are wholly exposed, the silliness of being betrayed there for everyone to gloat over. But not allowing myself to vent my fury meant that it coursed through my veins like poison, obsessive, destructive, until I

hated myself as much as I hated him. It was astonishing how persistent, how all-pervading, hatred became, how impossible any softening or forgiveness.

Clearly, I was not fit for any company; nor did I want any.

And then, or maybe and so, I fell head over heels in love, fighting against it every inch of the way. Perhaps it was because neither of us wanted or expected it, for it meant we did not try to hide anything from each other. Tormented by self-loathing, I found myself loved, by a man whose very foundation was honesty and honor. I think it was only then that I acknowledged what moral turpitude I had fallen into. He knew about that too, as well as trauma, but he had faced the consequences of certain attitudes with more careful thought than I, who was still messing about with the rights and wrongs and justifications of those consequences. My parfit gentil knight. It rather disgusts him that he is not immune to destructive emotions, but the certainty of his principles at least makes him recognize them for what they are, and prevent the consequences. And there, suddenly, was clarity, freedom without fear, acceptance.

One day he took me to a beach. The tide was out, miles away. He drew the sevenfold maze huge in the wet sand. I walked into it with my burden of grief and anger growing heavier with each step. Everything else disappeared. Spiraling inward concentrated the weight inside, until the full horror of the negation of life and love filled the whole of me. At the center I was a stone, a solid mass of death. Gerard Manley Hopkins knew:

> O the mind, mind has mountains; cliffs of fall
> Frightful, sheer, no-man-fathomed. Hold
>   them cheap
> May who ne'er hung there.

Slowly and painfully I forced myself to move again, walking the tight inner coils with trembling limbs, feeling sick. It seemed a piece of melodramatic self-torture, indulgence in self-pity about what had after all been the lot of many women. But each faltering step brought a lightening, as if in each layer of the maze I shed one of the layers of tragedy that had entombed me. As I realized what was happening I felt like Lazarus finding himself breathing again. Air fanned my cheek. The sand was golden, the mountains blue. I ran out, laughing.

We sat on our heels and watched the rising tide wash the maze away.

They said it would be possible to have another child, that having had one made another more likely in my condition; but I failed to conceive again. Wanting does not help. These accursed bodies women inhabit are not only bloody, but capricious and illogical. Why should our biology arrange that the terrified, traumatized child victim of a rapist get pregnant, doubly and trebly blighting her poor life, when two lovers who would happily devote their best to a child cannot make one? Was not the bond of heterosexual love a clever evolutionary device set up to give a child a decent two-parent start? Why should a man who desperately wants a child fall in love with one of the few women who cannot give him one? It is a problem that recurs.

I had said, If we are to part because of that, and despite the pain of parting I could not but respect your feelings and understand that it would be hopeless if you were unhappy, then let us at least make something from our feelings. Let us do something that only we could do, and only together; let us make an experience that will stay with us and enrich us, something that will reinforce our belief in love as a real and creative passion, even if we part straight afterward. For love in any of its forms, of person, child, art, or whatever you call God, is a celebration of the life force itself, imbuing our lives with a sense of the light and energy of creation, a channel into the inner I-am-that-I-am-ness that seeks no justification. It renders us as vulnerable as amoebae; we confound it with wishful thinking; our rationality cannot deal with it; yet without it, all becomes black and lifeless, or at best drab and mechanical. To stifle its creativeness because it inconveniences our other plans would be to deny a truth. We have to let it blossom in whatever way we can.

Being travelers, we had decided on this Quest, its hidden agenda revealed now only in its negation. For, far from producing fruit, it had led us to cripple a horse in the middle of nowhere, hate ourselves, and blow us apart.

Who the hell do you think you are, you incompetent failure of a woman? Damned. Doubly damned, drawing him into it too. Trebly damned: no manipulating your way out this time.

But the falling had stopped. We did not know it then, for we were so disoriented by the contortions we had gone through, but we had reached the center of the maze that had drawn us inexorably inward and stripped us naked. It was utterly still. All the whirling and falling had stopped. The sights that reached my eyes, the sounds that reached my ears, had no meaning. Even time stopped. There was only stillness.

Crawdaddies nibbled my toes.

Duchess, seeing me aware at last, sighed and splashed impatiently. I led her back over the dam. There had to be something positive. The best I could find was to mutter, "Sorry." It seemed pretty inadequate to describe how much I regretted having let him down, how much I regretted hurting him.

I cooked some bacon gently, skimming off the grease, for once blessing the fattiness of American bacon, and smeared it on a teased-out Tampax, the only cotton wool we had. I had not much hope of getting it on the gaping sore in Duchess's heel: she never let us touch that foot, and nailing a shoe on it had taken an extremely patient blacksmith an hour and a vast amount of tranquilizer. But I had to try.

She snatched up her foot the moment I looked at it, trying to hide it under her belly. Expecting her to lash out, I slapped the dressing on. To my surprise, she did not flinch; in fact, she stretched her leg back slowly, pressing the dressing on more firmly. She did not move while I bandaged it on; then she turned to touch me with her nose. I nearly burst into tears.

Emotions running wild again. No way to say anything: the alternative to stillness was turmoil. I walked along the top of the dam and up the hillside. A track led up through pine woods to join a dirt road. It branched again and again. I walked for hours, not thinking, just existing. Scores of elk were feeding in the forest. I could stalk them to within fifteen yards, and did so repeatedly. They seemed to know I meant them no harm. Horses, too, are acutely aware of the tension in our movements when we are intent on doing them harm. Exploring the network of trails, I finally found one that clearly led somewhere, which was a help, for our map stopped at the dam.

Face it. Make a plan. The horses cannot stay here: we have to move tomorrow morning, when the oats run out.

So, he goes: Load Rosie with all the gear he doesn't take, wrap a wet shirt around Duchess's leg, and limp her slowly. There is a ranger station somewhere: there'll be a telephone. Truck to Winslow. Sell the horses, pay the truck.

When I went back, at dusk, Rick had with great ingenuity made a rope fence at each end of the dam and turned the horses loose. Duchess was cheerfully hopping about on three legs. I told him my plan.

"I'm not going to leave you now," he said.

"I'll be all right, you know that. Anyway, you told me before, at the lake before Willow Creek, you didn't want us to carry on together. Age and babies."

"I'm not going to leave you now."

Later, I said: "We'll have to go on, you know."

"We can't, with Duchess. We'll go home."

"We can't do that either. Starr's not there for two days, and even if we could get a message to her we can't ask her to leave her dad. The horses will starve here. Duchess is hopping about anyway, so she might as well hop in a straight line. We'll make the ranger station in two days, even if we go really slowly."

He did not like it, but he agreed.

In the morning I went back up to the picnic site to try to find someone with a map. The only person there was the California blond.

"Hi," he simpered. "I'm so sorry I scared your little horsie."

 chapter seven

FREE FORWARD MOVEMENT is the first requirement of eques-
trianism: what is wanted is a horse that does not dither
about, drag its heels resentfully, get stranded in bushes, or
turn for home, but strides forward joyfully into the unknown.
Perhaps the years spent encouraging this attitude in young
horses has ingrained it in me, or perhaps it is simply that
moving feels better. We had tacitly abandoned what now
seemed like an impossible aim; our horizon had contracted to
one of finding good grass; but at least we could move freely,
if slowly, forward again.

The maze's inner circuits are tight, even on the way out.

One step after another, we crawled out of the marshy pit we
had put ourselves in. Exercise does not improve pulled liga-
ments, but Duchess grew no lamer as we strolled along slowly,
noble Rosie carrying all the gear. The forest changed again.
We passed beyond the canyons, whose runoff became chan-
neled into deep-cut creeks, and into drier forest. There was no
grass. Aspen and maple, both water-lovers, gave way to alliga-
tor-skin juniper, the huge ponderosa to smaller piñon pine.

The nuts hidden in the cones of piñon pine are much
prized by the Navajo, for they are rich and sweet; but they do
not ripen until late in the year. From their barren reservation
the Navajo used to make journeys of hundreds of miles on
foot to the high piñon forests, especially around the Grand
Canyon, to gather the nuts before the first snows. Some-

times, if the snow came early, they did not escape in time, and whole parties were lost. The ubiquitous pickup truck has not killed these traditional parties, but has made them safer and less exhausting.

You can tell a Navajo from a long way off by the straightness of his back. Traditionally, Navajo babies are kept in a cradle-board, a flat board shaped like an inverted U, to which the baby is strapped with a soft leather harness. When he is tiny he is swaddled comfortably, the back of his head supported by the board, his forehead protected by a wooden hoop. As he grows older his arms are left free, his toes allowed to touch the rim at the bottom of the board. He is propped upright in the corner of a room, able to watch his mother working and take an intelligent interest in what is going on, unlike our babies who so often lie on their backs staring at a blank ceiling, unable to see the source of the noises going on around them, or, for that matter, their mothers. The combination of secure swaddling and freedom to observe seems to suit them: Navajo babies are remarkably content and seldom cry. Perhaps the inevitable delay in unstrapping them before feeding teaches them patience from an early age, too. The constant support given to soft, growing bones molds them unmistakably: the back of the head is somewhat flattened, so that it grows broader, while the back becomes absolutely straight. The physique of a Navajo workingman is extraordinarily powerful, and judging from the way that old men walk, they do not suffer from back trouble even after a lifetime of heavy work.

There were two such figures working with a grader, the massive machine that resmooths the surface of a dirt road, as we came to a turning. They did not seem at all surprised to see our painful procession, but admired Rosie ("How much do you want for that horse?") and gave us water to soak Duchess's wrappings. We had seen a sign saying Dutch Joe, but they told us it was only a fire-watcher's tower; the ranger station was real enough but another day's journey away; and there was a good place to camp farther on.

Hart Springs was a prize: clear water running through a grassy glade, and a set of pens nearby. Rosie peered down a hole at the side of the road, scaring herself. The size of a badger hole, it was bottomless as far as all investigation could tell. A troll hole, perhaps.

Although Rick and I were still both numb and cautious, reeling from our contact with the inner void, the minutes and hours were creeping by, and we were creeping with them. Progress was being made. Life was going on. When disaster strikes and you see the whole edifice of your plans, and your apparent control over your future, come crashing to the ground, the natural reaction is to see only the chaos and failure. But as the dust settles and you take stock of the remains, you find you can arrange a stone here, a stick there, and lo! you have a fire, and a cup of tea. Refreshed, you notice you can construct somewhere to sleep; much improved, you see how imaginatively you can use debris; before long you are back erecting an Eiffel Tower. Every shoestring traveler knows how quickly triumph can turn to disaster; some of them bolt for the British Embassy before they consult their Kipling. For he was right: they are both imposters. Construction, destruction, it's all the same. We have control only of our attitude, not our fortune: the only thing we can congratulate ourselves on is having our eyes open at the right time.

When you travel with horses, you are forced to work your way through difficulties rather than doing a bunk. Abandoning the horses never occurred to us, although they would have been fine if we had turned them loose. Mustangs are so successful in the West that they are often regarded as vermin. There were cattle at Hart Springs, one a strange spotted creature that intrigued the horses: where cattle can exist, horses will do better. But it never crossed our minds. Nor did considerations about how long we were proposing to stay together, or what we would do if and when we managed to get to Winslow. We were here; there was sweet grass, and clear running water, and safe pens for the night. Duchess, though still very lame, was moving more easily, and the bacon grease was soothing her burn beautifully. Small things were plenty.

We camped in the pens. No sooner had we settled to sleep than Rosie shot into camp at a flat-out gallop, almost hurtling right into the tent, followed by Duchess. They were utterly panicked, high-stepping around in the dark with their tails in the air, snorting furiously. Duchess had lost her wet towel wrap; I thought she might have caught it in the fence and scared herself, but I could not find it, and she seemed perfectly calm about her leg. The affair was a mystery. We settled back to sleep. Almost immediately there were scuffles, galloping hooves, loud snorts, appeals for help; but no indication of what they needed protecting from. It happened again and again through the night. The only explanation seemed to be that the troll had emerged from his hole and with long, gray, warty fingers purloined Duchess's towel for some occult trolly purpose.

They were perfectly calm and innocent in the morning. We moved down to the spring for some good grazing and a caffeine jolt. Rick made one of the careful minimal fires he had been perfecting. Struck by the National Forest slogan, "Take nothing but pictures; leave nothing but footprints," he had become expert in digging tiny fire-pits just big enough for our pan, and recovering them with the turf he had removed. We really left no trace but hoofprints.

A jeep appeared. National Forest Law Enforcement, it said. The officer was burly, tanned, and mustached, with a broad, open face. We greeted him happily. Always assume you are innocent.

"S'pose I should tell you that fires are illegal in the forest, but I must say I can't fault your style," he said.

We hastened to douse the fire, but he stopped us, grinning. "What's that you got? Coffee?"

We scrambled to get him a cup. We make good coffee, the real stuff, boiled for half a minute. He sipped appreciatively, eyeing the horses. Rosie was tethered; Duchess, since she could not move fast, was loose.

"S'pose I should tell you it's illegal to graze horses loose in the forest. Oh, don't worry, leave her. Still, it's good to see you had the sense not to go camping in the pens."

It seemed to be a difficult conversation. I said, "They were dreadfully spooked by something last night."

"Lion," he said laconically. "There's been a couple 'round here for a while now. Guess you ain't familiar with lion, the way y'all talk."

We told him where we came from, our route from Prescott, the game we had seen, where we were heading, and our lack of a map.

"There weren't near so much game before the Forest Service put them tanks in," he said. "'Course, it's illegal to camp in a fenced tank, y'all know that by now, I'm sure. Otherwise them hunters'd just sit there until the game got so thirsty they'd have to get 'emselves shot. There weren't near so much grass a few years back, neither. When the settlers first moved out, the grass was stirrup-high to a tall horse, but the ranchers overgrazed it sump'n terrible. That's why Forest Service restricts them to four cows a section. They hate it." He grinned. "Say, how d'you work that li'l ol' fire? Sure makes good coffee; I'd like to see how."

We talked for hours; about the Forest Service's multiple-use scheme involving cattle ranching, elk-culling by paying hunters, camping, hiking, logging, fishing . . . the list went on; about Arizona history, Coronado's expedition from Mexico in 1541; about Apaches and felons, Whales and horses. The son of an Arizona rancher, he admired Rosie's robustness rather than Duchess's elegance. Disappointingly, he knew of no herbs that would help Duchess, nor indeed any useful plants at all. I am no great herbalist, but I do regularly use the commoner herbs that heal, and my lack of knowledge in this strange country had been bothering me. But Mike said flatly: "There ain't nothin' good in all this damned country. Ain't nothin' to eat between here 'n' Winslow, neither."

Our tiny fire kept churning out the coffee, and we were jangling with caffeine when he finally stood up.

"S'pose if I was to drop my map you'd just have to pick it up to save from littering, like the good folks you are." And he walked off, dropping the map.

"Thanks," we called.

"*Nada*. You bet."

The maze was unfolding. A thunderstorm broke and we went back to bed. We were wandering down the road, late in the afternoon, when various Forest Service trucks passed us, churning up the wet dirt into spatters.

"Knocking-off time," we said, and then, with growing comprehension, "They must be going to the ranger station." There was nowhere else except Winslow, sixty miles farther. We flagged down the next truck. A lugubrious Swedish face peered out, long-lipped with suspicion. Yes, he would take Rick and the bags to the ranger station, he said unenthusiastically. He seemed in too much of a hurry to say more. I undid Rosie's girth and pulled the heavy pack off, forgetting I had strapped it underneath with Duchess's rigging. Surprised by the straps clutching at her belly, Rosie shot off, bucking. The pack leaped from my arms and dragged after her as she tried to kick herself free. One saddlebag ripped, scattering rice and macaroni like confetti. Rick and I fell against each other, laughing, while the dubious face grew almost as long as Duchess's.

Eventually we untangled the wreckage, and Rick leaped in.

"Can she manage both horses by herself?"

"Oh yes," said Rick proudly, "she's a real expert with horses," and watched as I vaulted onto bareback Rosie, landed with my leg over Duchess's lead rope, and kicked the rope under Rosie's tail. She clamped her tail firmly over it, tucked her bottom down, and we bucked off down the road like a rodeo bronco act, dragging lame Duchess after us.

"You sure about that?"

But he was a kind man: he returned later to tell me that he had dropped Rick by some corrals a mile beyond the ranger station, which had closed for the night. It was dark by the time I neared the turning; I stopped to ask some Navajo wood-gatherers the way. They hid their beer cans behind their backs.

"How much you want for that horse?" they asked, pointing to Rose.

Having a pretty horse must be the best way to start a conversation with a Navajo: they all fancied Rose.

There were hunters already camped by the corrals, with two horses; but there was also a decent-sized paddock. Rick and I spent half the night fixing the fence before collapsing, exhausted. We did not dare to tempt the fates by admitting it, but we felt we were doing rather well.

Using all your Tampax to dress horses' heels can have severe disadvantages that characteristically only reveal themselves when you are least able to do anything about them. Rick went off to scout the way ahead while I, immobilized, lay in the tent in the rain all day, reading the book Starr had brought: *Hashknife Cowboy*.

The Hashknife outfit, so called because their brand was shaped like an inverted chopping blade, was the biggest ranch in Arizona: two million acres, 50,000 head of cattle.

When General Crook cleared the Apache, and Kit Carson the Navajo, onto reservations they made way for the railway. Built in 1880, it opened up the Arizona Territory, shipping settlers and prospectors in, gold and cattle out. Fortunes were made by sharp investors, and most Arizona towns were founded in 1882 or so. In return, the Territory granted the railroad company the land twenty miles each side of the line. Every alternate square-mile section remains public land, which means that if you own the sections each side, your

cattle also graze the public land between. Buy a million acres
at fifty cents an acre, as a group of easterners did in 1884, and
you control two million. The Hashknife outfit ran from
Mormon Lake to the New Mexico line, from the Navajo
reservation to the Mogollon Rim, with an overall stocking
rate of sixteen head per section, and a bunch of notoriously
wild cowboys manning it. The Hashknife was an empire,
with laws of its own.

But investors make poor ranchers: at a New York desk it is
hard to understand that a drought that wipes out a quarter of
your cattle can be followed by a two-day rain that drowns
half the rest. The Babbitts, a powerful Arizona family who
did understand, bought the Hashknife in 1901 and ran it
until the crash of 1932 put it in the hands of more investors.
They even enlarged it. The constant overstocking produced
financial rewards, but the toll on the land was immense.
Cattle do not crop grass: they wrap their tongues around it
and pull. In thin, dry soil they wrench it out by the roots,
leaving nothing to absorb the sudden, torrential rains. Heavy
feet crashing down water-eroded gullies only increases the
loss of topsoil. Grass stirrup-high to a tall horse is a legend of
the past.

Mack Hughes's book told of the effects: of cattle starving,
or dying in mud after rains, in the thousands; of the great
scab epidemic; of freezing winters and loco horses; of the
jokes and the whiskey stills. It also told me that by far the
best cure for rope-burns is bacon grease. The top of my head
was still open.

At nightfall I strolled over to my neighbors to ask for
water, and got beer instead. Doug, a wiry little old man, had
a huge blaze going and was carrying shovelfuls of fire over to
put under a massive cast-iron pot held up by his burly son.
The operation had an air of practiced skill, enhanced by the
peculiarly shaped shovel, the heavy concave lid of the pot,
and the long, hooked pole used for carrying the pot or lifting
the lid. It was a Dutch oven, the mainstay of chuck-wagon
cooking, as versatile as it is simple: you can bake bread or

biscuits, simmer chili and beans, or fry bacon in one.

"I've been reading about those things, but nobody ever describes them," I said. "I've got a book about the Hashknife. Do you know anything about it?"

"Yes ma'am, sure do." Doug grinned, pushing his hat back to scratch his head with a crablike gesture, then replacing it at the same becoming angle. All his movements were easy but limited, as if his body were a series of well-oiled levers: many a man who has spent his life working horses, and had most of his bones broken by them, moves like a crustacean. "Fact, I spent most of my life working for 'em."

Like most old cowboys, he was courteous and reserved; like many old people who know their own world intimately, he was rather baffled by confrontation with another. If I did not know what a Dutch oven was, what else might I be ignorant of? And on what points would I resent my ignorance, that western sin, being revealed? He did not want to hurt my feelings. Moreover, as he confessed the next day, he found my accent difficult to understand.

This admission sneaked out from beneath layers of assurance that it was no personal slight, nor was any offense intended. It is, though, something I forget, since in Britain I should be regarded as having "no" accent: for some reason it is easier to remember that your appearance is peculiar—for instance, that long blond hair is uncommon—or that your behavior is not usual for local women, than that your accent to a native English-speaker is incomprehensible even when you choose your words carefully. To me it seems strange that someone who can read the words "little" or "it isn't" should find it difficult to recognize them when pronounced as such, rather than as "li'l" and "ain't." Brian, his nine-year-old grandson, was even more perplexed.

I was beginning to wonder whether Doug wanted to have a conversation at all, when Rick arrived in a blaze of headlights. He had hitched a lift to Winslow with one of the rangers, bought a sack of oats, and dumped feeds off at various points.

"There's nothing out there," he said, "all the way."

"*Nothing?*"

"Nothing."

"What kind of nothing?"

"Nothing nothing."

"Nu'n," Doug confirmed, or perhaps corrected, handing us plates piled high with chili beans.

We had been too preoccupied with keeping our own psychological ships afloat and the mechanics of getting down the road to think much about poor dotty Duchess's neuroses. But it was here, browsing on the seedheads of grama grass, that she showed us unmistakably that she, too, had returned from the pits facing in the opposite direction.

Rick walked up to her when she was lying down. It sounds trivial. But horses do not lie down unless they feel safe (and they are less likely to lie down when they are sick, for they cannot get up quickly); they certainly do not let you walk up to them when they are lying down unless they trust you completely.

We looked at her afresh. Though lame, she was moving differently, fluidly. She was gaining weight. She shone like burnished copper, with a glow that came from under her skin rather than from our sketchy grooming. Her eyes were soft. We recalled that when Rosie had spooked at the troll hole, she had not tried to tear away from Rick but had pressed up to him for comfort. She would offer me her sore foot to dress. Paradoxically, it was the accident that had removed the last of her doubts and resistance, providing the final proof of what she had begun to suspect yet dared not conclude: that if she trusted us all would be well. From that day on, she was a changed horse, with that grand peacefulness of soul that is the birthright of horses and the blessing of those who crave their company.

But we still had a long way to go to Winslow, and she was still lame. It was not a pulled tendon but something higher up, which clicked at every step.

We stopped to say good-bye to Doug and Brian.

"Shoot, y'all ain't going yet? We thought we had neighbors . . . C'mon, y'all got time to chew the fat a while 'fore you leave."

And the questions came pouring out. They'd been thinking about us all night, and the more they thought, the more astonished they had become. We had to list all our gear, describe how we managed, what terrain we were used to, what Whales was like. Doug thought it was an island.

"Takes me three months to plan a week's hunting," he said.

"Seen any elk?" asked Rick.

"Big 'un this morning, but I didn't take a shot at him. If I shoot one now I'll have to go back. 'Druther have my week, elk or no elk."

This time the Dutch oven had coals piled in the lid. Out came a wonderful macaroni and cheese, browned on top and spiced with chili. Little Brian had caught a horny toad, a flat, spiky desert lizard, and was offering it morsels. He had made me a drawing of an elk.

Hashknife country. The juniper and piñon, with their Navajo wood-gatherers, thinned out; prickly pear began to appear for Rosie to practice her wisdom, then sagebrush and gopher holes, and we were on the open range.

Nu'n. Pale-brown nu'n, as far as the eye could see. It swept gently downward to the Little Colorado, sixty miles away, and rose the other side into a pink mirage. Apart from a lump called Chevelon Butte, it was empty, sighing softly, scented with sage. There was nothing but blue sky and brown earth, but the number of shades they managed to achieve was infinite. When you can see all of it, sky is thinner around the edges, the blueness above your head more solid than the clear margin where it touches the earth, the hues in between delicately graded.

This high, empty land neither stimulates nor demands: it allows. The actions of thinking things over, or having a conversation, which have finite time scales, are out of place in such infinity. Their very eagerness in trying to get somewhere, to reach a point, implies boundaries and features that do not exist. We had no sensation of movement, or of fatigue, as we walked hour after hour through the thin dry soil.

The sage-scented breeze soughed through our brains and left them as clean as the white bones we passed. Was it merely

horny toad.

our organic response to this vast landscape that made our tortured tangles evaporate into clear air?

Now, it seems to me that this is where I realized that we had been inexorably led inward in ever-decreasing, deepening circles, and just as inexorably led outward again, relinquishing our burdens, into cleaner, stronger freedom; and that all we had to do was put one foot after another on the path we had been shown, or that we had designed for ourselves. It seems to me that I knew, suddenly and certainly, that from here on it would be plain sailing; but this is now, and at the time I probably had no such idea, ideas being altogether too concrete. At the time, I was probably singing, mindlessly, "Don't fence me in," for all I know.

The sun rolled slowly over the sky and down the other side, producing colors of such delicate loveliness as to make you realize you had been smiling for hours. The brown of the earth grew deeper, ruddier, until we were walking over a blood-red sea under a violet sky. The great ball touched the level horizon and slid down over it. Nowhere else is what gives us life so apparent. The air chills immediately; the earth does not retain its warmth long either.

It was dark when we found the roadside loading chute where Rick had left the oats; but there was no water for the horses, though we had canteens for ourselves. The map showed a ranch a few miles away, but there was no light; yet even a deserted ranch implies water nearby. The gate half-way up the track was locked, the fence impassable. Rick disappeared for hours, returning with our plastic bucket full of water. And the horses refused it.

A sky full of stars, and coyotes running, their clear chiming cries swelling and fading. Boundlessness of body and soul.

Dawn begins long before sunrise. At that altitude, the dry air is as sharp as a knife, not with the shivery cold of damp climates, but a cold that quickens your brain while the rest of you toasts in your sleeping bag. To the east, the sky begins to

glow deep purple, and the stars fade. From the horizon the colors seep upward: violet, turquoise, green, yellow, pink, and white. By the time the golden rim appears, all the color has leached upward. The ground reddens. Slowly, majestically, the daily miracle begins, pouring its blessed warmth into you.

Nomads always pitch their tents facing east. The splendor of a sunset can be missed, but not that blessing of dawn. We have lost our ways of saluting it: in soggy Britain we can seldom see it, let alone celebrate it from afar. But in the piercing quality of desert air, where all is clear, you feel the loss as if you had forgotten how to greet people properly.

Duchess again refused the water. It smelled all right to me, but in a dry climate a horse must have strong reasons for not drinking for twenty hours. I poured it away, but Rosie managed to catch a couple of swallows before it hit the ground.

I set off alone, leading Duchess and riding Rosie, while Rick hitched down the road with the packs. Anybody passing was bound to go to Winslow, for there was nowhere else to go. I was pleased at the idea of being alone in that immensity, but the horses were as uncooperative as only horses or overtired children can be. They were both dehydrated, of course: when I pinched a fold of skin on their necks it did not snap back into place, but sank back slowly; they both probably had splitting headaches. Even so, they were monstrously sulky. Both wanted to go first, and hung back if they were second. When I forced them to walk side by side they argued with each other. If I let go of Duchess she made off westward, probably smelling water. When I spoke to them about it (any horse that knows you as those two did us understands your tone of voice perfectly well) they simply sighed, pouted, and dug their heels in.

After a couple of hours they perked up, and soon even I could smell water. It was two miles away, in a huge circular steel tank. They drank and drank, pawing at the sides of the tank. I climbed in, took off my shirt, and washed them with it; though it was not hot, I thought they would feel better. But there was nothing to eat: horses do not eat sagebrush or dirt, and there was nothing else except drifting tumbleweed.

We strolled along, dripping in the dust. From miles away

a coyote loped straight toward us, catching their attention. As he drew nearer I saw he was not a coyote but an antelope, moving in the same tireless canter. He was rangy, belly tucked up with thirst and hunger, not fat and sleek like the forest deer and elk. But he was a dandy little fellow, earth-brown on top and shimmering white below, from his throat to his stubby tail. I stood stock-still between the horses, and he loped past only a few feet away, big dark eyes unworried, the twirls of his horns glistening in the sunlight, not bothering to deviate from his arrow-path to the tank. He seemed to drink forever.

"There's more food for lunch by the black tank," Rick had said.

"Which black tank?"

"You'll see it; you can't miss it."

I could not, even from ten miles away. It was absurd: a massive boiler of a tank, perched on a mound in the middle of nu'n, with a tap that dwarfed the horses. The effect was surreal. Standing on the mound increased the horizon: like a fairytale land, the pink and gold stripes of the Little Painted Desert shimmered in the heat, hanging above the brown of the range. Little clouds scudded over it so that it vanished and reappeared, different each time. Could any of this be real?

We set out again happily, but within half an hour Rosie's greedy gulps of bad water that morning started to take effect. She got diarrhea badly, frighteningly. Horses can dehydrate very rapidly; salmonella and other bugs can kill within hours. The map showed a line of windmills, whose lazy silver blades turn air into water, leading in roughly the right direction. They were only three or four miles apart, but far from the road, the only possible source of help. There was no sign of the telltale puff of dust from a car, though, and anyway, I could not leave the horses without tying them to a tank: we would never find them again.

We turned away from the road, heading for the nearest beacon. Cautiously we crept from tank to tank, keeping Rosie as waterlogged as possible, though it poured out of her at a horrible rate. It was an extraordinary day, the golden mirage dancing on the horizon, the vast openness of the range, the sense of purity and cleanness, the solitude, and the nearness of death. We passed bleached skulls with huge sweeping horns. I cuddled Rosie and called her a brave little soul, and she listened with half an ear while I sang.

At sundown we reached the last tank, drenched in blood-red light. Grass glowed an unearthly green against the vermilion dust. Rosie tried to climb into the tank, then lay down, groaning, eyes closed. I stood alone on the surface of a dying, empty planet.

"I refuse to believe it," I said aloud.

She winked at me, leaped to her feet, frisked around merrily, and tucked into the grass. She was as right as rain after that.

We swung back onto the roadside after dark, for there was no other way of knowing where to go. I had let go of Rosie and was walking with Duchess, when Rosie neighed ahead of us. When we caught up with her she was standing by an old campfire, smelling it, peering and calling into the dark. She was looking for Rick. He was always by a campfire, wasn't he? And our herd was not complete without him.

It was she, too, who spotted his fire a mile off the road, hours later. He was camped in the corner of a four-section paddock near a ranch, thoroughly disgruntled. For once, western hospitality, usually wholly generous, had failed. He had said he was aiming for the ranch but the driver giving him a lift had dumped him and the gear at the roadside, so he had lugged the gear in two trips, four miles in all, to the ranch. The woman there had been positively hostile, but had at last allowed him to camp. We gave the horses their feed and debated whether to tie them all night.

"They'll stay around," I said confidently. "We've been going for twelve hours, Rosie's bushed and Duchess is still lame, and there's more food here. They'll stay."

Ten minutes later they kicked up their heels and galloped off into the night.

Salaaming the rising sun, my god if ever I had one, I walked three miles through a rose-pink dawn past sculpted outcrops of golden sandstone, soft as soap, to retrieve them. They were in the farthest corner, where Rosie was playing cow pony with a bunch of steers she had pinned against the fence. They were immensely pleased with themselves and bucked joyfully all the way back to camp. Duchess limped at a trot, but galloped well.

We found Rick chatting to the elderly rancher and his son, the warmth of whose welcome puzzled us further. We unraveled this mystery a week later: the men had been away for the night and the woman, an employee, had been thrown into confusion by her fear of this strange-talking, filthy tramp, her embarrassment at being asked for hospitality that she felt was not hers to give, and her shame at turning him away unfed into a paddock. Poor *señora,* you did fine.

Sparse, withered grass replaced the sagebrush as we dropped toward the Little Colorado. Rick, leading Duchess, was suddenly incensed with rage.

"I came here to ride, not to lead a lump of dogmeat."

"Then ride," I said, handing him Rosie. Still fuming, he climbed aboard, then broke into shouts of laughter as they lolloped about.

"She's Tank Engine Thomas! Chug-a-chug puff! No wonder you're so cheerful."

It was true: her naïve optimism had constantly lifted my spirits when I rode her. As a novice rider, it seems that achieving harmony with your horse is an unattainable dream. The harder you try, the more your directedness alienates him. It is letting go, feeling the horse infiltrate and extend you until his movement becomes yours, that allows your purpose to become his. Once you have learned to banish tension and worry the moment you hit the saddle, the reversal rapidly becomes automatic. The horse seduces you into his worldview. Thus Rosie transformed Rick from half a cripple into a merry fool in a trice, and we rolled downhill to Winslow. Rick's recon had produced the promise of a bath . . .

 chapter eight

AN EAGLES HIT ALBUM has a song, "Take it Easy," that describes a hitchhiker's stop on the famous Route 66: "Standing on a corner in Winslow, Arizona . . ." It delighted the inhabitants of Winslow. Their town has been immortalized in song. The Halls of Fame include Winslow. Their only postcard shows a corner, believed to be That Historic Corner, though no one is standing on it.

Winslow is a railroad town, five miles long and four streets wide. We reckoned it had to be that long or they might not have fitted a whole train into it.

There is something almost intolerably romantic about American freight trains. (I remember Rick looking at me as if I had lost my last shred of sanity when I raved about them, but one glimpse won him over.) No one who has read American novels or heard American folk songs can have escaped the grandeur, the hopes, and the despairs epitomized by those endless clanking boxcars, those lonely wailing hoots. An American freight train can be two miles long, pushed and pulled by up to half a dozen locomotives. Snaking across that vast continent, through swamps and forests, over mountains and deserts, it takes miles to reach more than walking pace with its medley of contributions: Southern Pacific, Rock Island Line, Cotton Belt, Santa Fe. There is plenty of time for the hobo to climb aboard, shin up the little ladder, and drop into a world of dreams: "Bound for glory," sang

Woody Guthrie. All the energy and diversity, the ingenuity and color, of that extraordinary country travel together in those trains.

Two stopped end to end take a lot of riding around. The only other way was under, via a tunnel regularly charged by forty-ton Kings of the Road or by a narrow, steeply stepped pedestrian corridor, neither very suitable for horses with the winds of the high range still fanning their ears. Rick rode across the tracks to the driver of one train and discussed the state of various nations, the Gulf War, electoral systems, and rainfall before they waved good-bye. It was a quarter of an hour before the last car had passed.

The back alleys of the town were full of Navajo in blue denim, most of them either drunk or very drunk. Indians get drunk easily. Whether this is entirely due to physiological differences, which certainly exist, or because the point of drinking is to get drunk is difficult to say. Gray Elk, a Sioux, says he does not understand the attitude of the white man, who when drinking tries to conceal its effects: if you enjoy being inebriated, why fight its pleasant muzziness? But alcoholism is a real problem, and on most reservations, including Navajo and Hopi, alcohol is banned. Winslow being the first town south of the reservation, any Navajo who wants to get drunk heads straight there. He does not become aggressive, rowdy, or sick, merely rather unsteady on his feet and less unapproachable or, as we found, liable to embrace passing horses like long-lost blood brothers. When he is very drunk, he lies down wherever he is and sleeps it off.

It is the least unsociable way of getting drunk in public that I have ever seen, but it does not impress the local whites, who tend to assume that all Indians are permanently drunk. This is about as fair as judging the whole British nation from the behavior of hooligans at a soccer match.

Still surprised at having made it this far, we called in at the horse-feed store, where the two Navajo boys who had helped Rick before greeted him with delight and promised to deliver more food. We were to camp in some dusty pens lent by a man whose blue eyes seemed to shine with inner radiance. I found myself gawking at him like a child.

But our first priority was Duchess. The only vet was at the extreme other end of town, five miles away. Choked by the smell of exhaust fumes, I followed Route 66 past innumerable Burger Kings and Pizza Huts to describe the accident and her symptoms minutely to a vet who could not stop giggling at my accent. I was scared that, like Rick, he would prescribe an immediate return to the meat sale, but his diagnosis was unequivocal: the only possible injury that fitted was a wrenched ligament in the stifle, the knee joint at the top of the leg. A visit was unnecessary. Rest, especially early on, would have made it worse: the cure was slow, steady walking exercise, the more the better. I almost cried. It felt as if a great hand had laid itself comfortingly on my shoulder, like the blessing sun rising over darkened land.

We feasted in a merry Mexican café.

"Rick?"

"Hmm."

"What are we doing?" Since the accident we had thought only of getting to Winslow and the vet. The possibility of Duchess's continuing had been unthinkable.

"Going to Hopi."

Of course. But between us and the end of this maze lay some seventy miles of desert and semidesert, most of it Navajoland. How we were to cross it remained a mystery. To the Navajo and Hopi officials we met, there was no problem. The road was on the map. There was no food and little water, but if we wanted to go that was fine.

The Anglos shook their heads at our innocence. Among the varieties of prejudice we picked up were: the Navajo were lazy ("they run all those pickups on welfare"), thieving ("if it ain't nailed down it ain't stealing"; "they'll steal your horses"), hostile ("take one step off the highway and they'll shoot: they shoot first and ask questions later"), and dirty ("all that stuff about ecology is bullshit: they throw trash everywhere"). One

might equally say that they are noncompetitive, do not believe in personal possessions, are not overanxious to befriend
supercilious tourists whose grandparents might have massacred theirs, and cannot afford to be caught with an empty beer
can. It became obvious that the less people knew of the
Navajo, the readier they were to condemn.

Besides, I had been to their northern land before, and had
been invited to ride up the Canyon de Chelly with them on
the strength of my ability to pronounce the sound written in
Welsh as "ll," which occurs in Navajo too. They had a fine
line in poker-faced teasing of a subtlety wholly foreign to the
majority of Americans, and produced for me a starkly mad
ex-racehorse whose antics, once I had proved my ability to
stay on, they encouraged by trying to rope his tail every time
we whizzed past. This brief encounter left me with the impression that they were simply sick of humorless, brash tourists, but gave no indication as to how they would react to
being asked for horse feed.

Rick returned from a fact-finding expedition shaken. He
had met his first Hopi, in a bar: a young woman, with three
silent men, one a Navajo swigging from a bottle of Thunderbird he kept under the table. The young woman stared,
unblinking, straight into his eyes. She said immediately that
what he would find at Hopi was not what he was looking for,
that he did not know where to stop, and would get in deeper
than he thought or was prepared for. She thought he was a
Snake. She herself was a Rabbit. She stroked his arm, eyes
locked on his, and asked him to her room. He was thoroughly spooked, feeling a need for caution he had not felt
before, though about what he had no inkling. He was also
disconcerted by the impression she was a bad lot. Certainly
she was drinking fairly heavily, but her blank stare had an
aura of cocaine about it, though he hesitated to make the
obvious inference. Everything we had read or heard about
the Hopi suggested they had great spiritual awareness. He
feared what that penetrating gaze had seen within him, and
was uneasy about being a Snake.

I looked up the clan: it is linked to the Snake Mound in Ohio, feathers, seashells, Tuzigoot, and the great plumed serpent Quetzalcoatl himself. It did not seem so bad to me, though I did not know what to make of the rest. If she had had any perception she would have seen that there was no need to frighten him: he is quite self-critical enough already.

The best baths are those taken after two months' desert traveling, especially when provided by people like Fyrn who believe in gilding the lilies of luxury. I lay soaking, envying the easy charm with which Rick can make almost anybody laugh, before spending as long trying to scour the bathroom of sand, tumbleweed seeds, and a hitchhiking beetle. My clothes reeked of horse.

Ron, Fyrn's husband, was a quiet, correct man who kept startling me over a stupendous dinner. He was a prison officer. I could not imagine how anyone so gentle could cope with the violence of American criminals. He said that avoiding confrontation, his specialty, tended to defuse most situations, though he had been knifed a couple of times. Most arrests, in Winslow, were for drugs: a couple of dozen a week, which, given the size of the place, seemed to imply that half the population must be doing time or high.

"We don't bother about personal pot," he said. "It's harder stuff we're after. They often get off with plea bargains. Most of 'em are just silly, but some are real bad, *real* bad."

"Why so much drugs? Winslow seems a mild sort of place."

"No different from anywhere else. There's such a pressure to compete, to succeed. America's based on it. Some of 'em can't see themselves making it good so they take the easy way out."

"It must make child-rearing difficult."

"Yeah. My son, now, he shot himself."

Steak stuck in my jaw at this calm revelation.

"He was sixteen. I had too high expectations of him. You want your son to be more than you. I just put too much pressure on him. Took me a while to come to terms with it." His movements were soft and quiet, musing.

What would I have done to my son? How would I have prepared him for a society whose materialism and competition I do not cherish? Is there not enough arbitrary tragedy in the world without our engineering more? My head imploded. I longed for the desert.

Neighbors called in to meet us: a man who was as determined to impress his redneck opinions on us as his vivacious, dark-haired wife was to explain that he did not really mean them. We ran through the gamut of anti-Indian prejudice, against a chorus of muttered protests from the others, before he started on horses.

"When a horse does wrong I spank him good," he said, puffing out his chest. "Whuppin's all they understand."

"I'd say they learn a lot better from praise and reward," I said.

Mary defended him: "He's not really so hard, you know. He's always pettin' on 'em and givin' them sweetfeed when he works them."

He looked embarrassed.

"I'm sure you do, or you wouldn't be as good a trainer as you say you are," I needled.

"Sure I do," he admitted uncomfortably.

"Then why say spanking's the only thing they understand? People get the wrong end of the stick, like the boy who beat up Duchess. He was taking his attitude from people who talk like you do even though they act otherwise."

"Some folks'll never be horsemen anyways, however you talk."

The Minnetonka, a bar and Indian gift shop out of town, toward the reservation, was recommended to us. Julie, tough and cheerful, waved our horses in the direction of pens, and we went for a couple of beers. The place was throbbing with good music, bobbing hats, and laughter. Among the regulars, Julie said, was a man who taught in a Navajo school, but he did not come in that night. The others investigated these strangers on their patch. Dudley, a sweet-smiling railroad man with his engineer's cap turned back-to-front, tried to teach me the Texas swing; Hod boasted that his apprentice-ship as town drunk was almost complete; a bunch of young ranchers spat streams of tobacco juice into glasses containing tissues, which Julie had served up with the drinks; three riotous forty-year-old divorcées convinced themselves of their freedom with shrieks of raucous laughter; J. D., Julie's brother, recognized a soul mate in Rick. The atmosphere after our solitary sobriety was too seductive, and we ended up drinking half the night with J. D. in a storeroom before crashing out in an empty trailer behind the bar. Just a couple of beers . . .

Recovered, we returned a couple of days later to meet Gordon the schoolteacher, in his alternative role as Minne-tonka encyclopedia and scribe. Seeing us coming, he reached into his pocket for a piece of paper covered in lists.

"When Julie told me what you wanted to do I thought it was impossible," he said, dispensing with any preliminaries. He was elderly, with a slightly pedantic air. "But four days' ride will do it. Now, the first day you follow the road to the trading post, where they will put you up. The second day you go to Felix and Susie. They are good people and work at the school in Seba Dalkai, where I teach. Felix also has horses. The third day brings you to the school . . ."

He had planned it out, every step; telephoned people, arranged where to stay, food for the horses. We were over-whelmed.

"This is extremely kind of you."

"Not at all. The children will be pleased to meet you and hear about Wales: we'll work you hard, all day."

"What do you teach?"

"Sixth grade. I don't pretend to teach them anything: we just exchange information. No, not another, I have to go. Don't lose that paper."

We celebrated Minnetonka-style. Dudley, disappointed by my inability to stick to the correct steps, steered me to the back half of the dance floor, which, he said, was the old headquarters of the Hashknife. Suddenly there was an up-

roar. Black Chas, a railroad man, exasperated by the cowboys' jibes about his skin and ancestry, burst out shouting at
the top of his impressive voice.

"So who do you think opened this country up? 'Twarn't
you good-for-nothin' cowboys, it was us *blacks*. Ain't you
ever heard of the Buffalo soldiers?"

"Yee-ha," they whooped. "Attaboy, Chas!" But their efforts
had succeeded, and they could afford to stop their teasing,
whose crudity, despite its good nature, had revolted me. As
they soothed him with Wild Turkey, I talked to a young
Navajo woman huddled miserably in a corner. Her whole
attention was on her handsome boyfriend as he moved around
the bar. He was irritated by her possessiveness, and showed it.

"Don't worry," I said, "he'll come back. If you try to keep
him on a leash, he'll only want to escape."

"That's what he says made him break up with me before.
We've only just got back together. But I'm scared he'll leave
me here." Her eyes rolled. She was as shy as a deer, but her
agitation slowly left her. As soon as we were in deep conversation, it was he who was hovering around. She held my
hand and giggled.

The calf broke from the chute pursued by a thunderbolt of
1100 pounds of horse. Rope whirled, lanced forward, snapped
tight. The calf kicked, but the rider was already on the
ground and running, thongs in hand, his horse backing away
to keep the rope taut. Hand circled swiftly, twice; the calf lay
bound; the man threw his arms up. Dust settled slowly, red
under the arc lights.

"Ten seconds," droned the announcer.

Rodeo. It was a small and quiet one, but I was glad for Rick
to see it. The horses jogging quietly by, ropes trailing behind
them; their explosive leap from the chute; the flurry of dust
under arc lamps; the proudly worn prize buckles on heavy,
decorated belts; and the sea of hats: these are an integral part
of the West, though for the most part the competitors are
weekend, rather than working, cowboys.

Their horses, too, are far from the typical wiry working cow ponies. Rodeo quarter horses are massive, big-bottomed, and wise. Between turns they do not fret; they go back to sleep. You cannot believe that the rearing monsters in the chutes are the docile plugs that dozed beside you a minute before. They will doze, leap, doze, and leap all evening, after which they often hop into the back of pickup trucks and spend the night conversing amiably with each other, parked outside a bar. Their temperament, mild and forgiving, is enhanced by the unhurried western attitude and the style of riding, which allows a horse the freedom to use his head and balance in a way that is most natural to him.

Europeans are often aghast at the savage western bit; they fail to notice that the bit is seldom used, for the horse can be stopped and turned by balance. The bit is merely a reminder that there is an imperative to respond to tiny cues, just as the noise of spurs is enough to remind the horse to leap forward at the slightest leg squeeze. Of course there are idiots like Duchess's ex-owner who abuse these tools, but the average western horse has an easier time being ridden than the constantly pushed, pulled, and nagged European horse, and he shows it.

We looked at the program. The first page welcomed us and said:

> Heavenly Father, we thank you for the many blessings you have bestowed upon us. We ask that you would protect the human and animal athletes at this Rodeo. We pray that you would bless the time, energies, and monies put forth by those who have labored to make this event a success. We thank you for this contest and the other tests we have in this life. In the name of our Lord, Jesus Christ, Amen.

The next events were team roping, where two cowboys rope the head and heels of a calf, stringing him out like an unwilling sausage; bulldogging, where a cowboy throws himself from his horse onto a fleeing steer, and by wrenching its neck sideways, wrestles it to the ground; and bronc riding. You have to stay on a bronc for eight seconds to gain points according to the bronc's rating. Rodeo broncs are not wild horses; many are perfectly tame, albeit unridable, especially when the bucking strap is tightened around the belly. Bucking is their work, with luck only a few seconds once or twice a month. One of them, a shock-maned bay mustang, dumped his rider in two corkscrew leaps and ran straight up to the cowboys whose job it is to lift the rider off if he survives the ride. The pony offered them his back so they could unhook the bucking strap, wheeled, and galloped back into his pen. Easy work. Wise guy. He was resting before his ex-rider had limped from the ring, dusting off his pants.

In a heavily barricaded crush another rider lowered himself cautiously, watched by wary helpers. He took a strap, wrapped it carefully around his left hand, settled himself on the unseen, shifting beast, raised his right hand, and nodded. The gate sprang open and a huge bull, elegant and enraged, burst forth. Horses tend to hump their backs, bouncing and twisting stiff-legged; bulls do handstands in circles, often corkscrewing as they go, so with luck the rider is thrown clear enough to run for safety before the monster bucks around to face him. For the unlucky, the clowns, old riders themselves for the most part, divert the bull's attention, dancing mockingly or somersaulting in their flapping clothes in extraordinary displays of courage, timing, and taurine psychology. I have seen an old man on his knees, tiny before a pawing, rumbling bull, mimicking his sideways swipes of dust until the creature charged, surprising himself in meeting thin air as the man launched himself sideways. Though the tips of the bull's horns are sawn off, he can still smash and toss; and his agility compared with that of a domestic bull is like that of an Olympic athlete compared with a pregnant housewife.

"Mad," said Rick as another ton of humpbacked Brahma-Angus, red-eyed with fury, threw its back end above its head.

The man, falling, could not release his strap, but was dragged backward while the beast bucked around and around, lashing out at him.

There are easier ways to lose money.

A couple of days later Duchess had truly recovered, but our farewell beer or two at the Minnetonka led to a numbed late start. As we headed out of town past the laundromat, with its crowds of brightly dressed Navajo women busily washing, a truckful of grinning faces beamed at us: Susie and her children, with whom we were to stay. Our elation was damped, though, by the difficulty we had in persuading the horses across the bridge over the Little Colorado, another dirty trickle in a wide wash; the bridge over the highway scared them so much they had to scuttle down the white line, equidistant from the horrors on each side. We turned off the road onto open range again, and set our faces toward the dark buttes and mesas jutting from the immense sweep of golden land rising before us. We were going to make it after all.

We loped along for mile after mile in easy comfort; at least, Rick did. Rosie's canter was short-strided and bouncy, and she huffed and puffed at every step. The day was full of joy and sweetness. The horses were fit and fresh, glad to be on open land again, where the going was easy underfoot and the air light and lively after Winslow's smog. Soft in this sharp clarity, the tawny land rolled on forever in ripples like the muscles on a lion's back.

The sun crawled slowly around to our left and hung, a flattened red ball, above the purple peaks of the San Francisco Mountains on the distant horizon; then it slid down as suddenly as a sinking ship. We were still miles from our destination. Occasional cars gave us the line of the road, parallel to the old track we were following by starlight. We could see their lights for what seemed like hours before they passed. A single static light by the road had to be our trading post; but we were puzzled by a straight line of lights behind it. I started counting the seconds from when a car passed the

trading post to when it passed us: eight miles, five, three . . .
We jogged along the sandy track under a myriad of stars,
listening to distant coyotes. As we drew nearer the landing-
strip lights, it became obvious they were not horizontal but
vertical, rising sky-high above us on some unseen scaffold-
ing. It was a microwave tower, beaming out telephone conversations from executives stuck in traffic jams. Sand had
blown against the side of the maintenance shed in an elegant
curve.

The trading post was a small supermarket and gas station, where another immense meal awaited us. Ernie, the
owner, was as disparaging about the Navajo as anyone we
had met, though his wife, Doreen, put up a spirited defense
of them.

"Trouble is," he said, sprawling on his couch after a hard
day, "they don't want to work."

"C'mon, Ernie, you know most of our help's Navajo."

"Yeah, and they leave."

"Some of them have been with us for years. And the
others—well, people do leave jobs like that. There's always
a turnover."

"I don't want to work at things I don't enjoy," Rick and I
said together.

"Then you won't get anywhere, or have anything."

Space, time, freedom to celebrate life, to wonder and
think; to grow; to follow the four directions to their limits,
investigate potentials; to be here, even if dependent on your
hospitality, Ernie. Even that is not just taking, for it gives you
the opportunity to be generous, which you enjoy.

We slept in a bed, uneasy between vertigo and claustro-
phobia.

In the morning Rick and Ernie drove to Felix's, twenty-
five miles away, with the packs, while I watched that great
racehorse Secretariat on the television. His huge stride
made him seem a unique species: like a cheetah, he could
dislocate his front end, launch it forward until his feet hit
the ground, hinge himself together again, and coil his back-

side under himself ready for another launch. He looked so slow, yet he soared past his brisk opponents like a swan past a swallow. Superhorse. Watching the Prix de l'Arc de Triomphe in a curtained trailer in the middle of that great pale plain made me laugh.

A couple of miles up the track we were in the Little Painted Desert. The rolling range suddenly stopped, its delicate superstructure of dust and sparse grass too precarious to maintain. Crumbling craters opened up vistas of salty, shimmering white shot through with stripes of maroon, yellow, rose-pink, and mauve. We plunged into the humps and canyons of the fairytale land we had glimpsed from the black tank. Though parched and lifeless except for the buzzards hoping overhead, and flitting lizards like miniature dinosaurs, the desert was strangely cool as we swung, silent with wonder, through softly eroded gullies of unlikely pastel hues.

The creator had been trifling idly when he poured these colored sands, nurturing the seed of the mania that inspired the larger Painted Desert farther north into wilder and wilder extravagancies of silly things you can do with sand (ridiculous riots with rock was a later, bolder phase). This was mere child's play; but it was nevertheless so peculiar as to make you feel you had been transported to the face of another planet. Visiting these fantasy lands in a car is wholly different from traversing them on horseback, for your environment still includes your car. However far you wander from it, the knowledge of it anchors you to familiar realities. On foot, pleasant progress would be threatened by the danger of staring yourself to death, or nagging yourself to reach somewhere less lethal. But on a horse, you glide along effortlessly, able to stare and wonder as well as move. The queerness of being somewhere that cannot be called land, for land implies a clothing of life, nor the skeleton of land, for it lacks the form of bare bones, but is a kind of junkyard of the powdered elements of that skeleton, can be allowed to absorb you without impeding you.

I would have liked to stay there, to watch the shifting light from dawn to dusk play arpeggios on the scale of colors, and see what visions emerged; but we were unprepared. We padded on through a giant's sandbox of sagging candy-striped shades, past glistening outcrops of brilliant white where rust-red sandstreams ran downhill in cataracts. Below wind level, it was unnaturally still and quiet.

buttes + mesas in Navajoland

Presently we remembered the camera and scrabbled in the packs for it, but even holding it had the usual effect of making us look for photos instead of observing what was before us. Why committing images to celluloid should prevent them imprinting themselves on a grander scale on our neural networks must be the effect of the attention filter known as search image. We were not, despite our original intentions, dutiful photographers, being too immersed in experience to remember the camera; where we did, my memories are of snapshots, either taken or dismissed, framed in black and usually without accompanying smells, sounds, and feelings. Where we forgot it, the scene is unbounded, the visual part inextricable from the impressions of other senses. I do not think this is wholly due to my incompetence with a camera, for many proper photographers seem incapable of describing scenes except by reference to photos they have taken.

The shifting, swirling colors gradually gave way to paler, more uniform rock, which stayed still long enough to entertain withered scraps of grass. We pulled up a long slope onto the surface of the earth, and found our way barred by a stout fence. It was only by climbing the highest rise that we spotted a track leading through it.

The gate was padlocked. We lifted it off its hinges, went through, replaced it carefully.

We were in Navajoland.

chapter nine

THERE ARE A QUARTER of a million Navajo, of whom 150,000 live on a reservation rather larger than Wales. Relatively speaking, they are newcomers to Arizona: when Coronado rode through in 1541, en route from Mexico City to Kansas (where he fell off his horse jousting), he made no mention of Navajo or Apache; the Querecho Indians he met buffalo hunting in New Mexico were possibly Apache on a southerly jaunt. To him the area was populated by Pueblo groups: Zuni, Hopi, Tiwa, Acoma, and others, peaceful corn growers terrified by the appearance of fierce, hairy-faced white men mounted on animals that ate people.

Apache and Navajo (the Navajo were first called *Apache de navajo*, the Apache of the knife) are Athabascan speakers; all other Athabascans live much farther north, mostly in Canada. Nomadic hunters, they moved south, carrying their possessions on dogs, until, around 1650, some groups reached down into New Mexico and Texas. It was here that they got horses, first from Mexican tribes in whom horse possession had slowly been spreading north, and then through mounted raids on each other and Spanish ranchers. For a couple of hundred years they, and the Plains Indians who took up horses after them, had an enormous amount of fun.

To the half of the world that does not suffer from the stuff, testosterone looks as dangerous as any banned drug. A young man whose veins are pumped full of it is liable to succumb to a terrible urge to prove it makes him more virile than anyone else. In nomadic groups, whether from the American or Asian steppes, acquisition of horses naturally led to mounted raiding as an expression of high spirits and valor. Swooping down on a camp at full gallop, touching enemy braves to humiliate them, driving off their horses, taking their prettiest women, retelling it all over a campfire at night: what could be more glamorous? This was not warfare, but surprise rugby: nomads have no concept of land ownership, nor use for the encumbrances of material luxury. Their minimal possessions may be beautifully wrought and decorated, but they are strictly functional. To most North American tribes, the only point of acquiring property is to be able to throw a party or ceremony and give it all away: it is troublesome, demoralizing stuff. The aim of a raid was not conquest or killing, but point-scoring and fun. It got rough sometimes, but so does rugby.

To the European peasants who crawled across the continent in their wagon trains, land ownership and material possessions represented not only freedom from oppressive overlords but precisely what wars were waged over. They replied with a different game. By the time the Indians had realized that the rules included massacring unprotected women and children, using germ warfare, destroying their revered food source, and confining survivors in wildlife parks, it was too late. War not only killed and dispossessed them: attempting to understand the principles underlying it overturned their whole value system, leaving them clueless in an alien world.

That the Navajo survived better than most is a tribute to the adaptability that has always been their strength. They suffered as badly as any. After Kit Carson slaughtered their women and children in the Canyon del Muerte in 1863, the horrified remainder of the tribe declared they wanted no more atrocities. When they laid down their arms, ten thousand were marched 350 miles to the Bosque Redondo, eastern New Mexico. Some fifteen hundred died on the "Long

Walk." Even their inventiveness could not match the bleakness of the small reservation, and many more died. Four years later the survivors were returned to their canyons and plateaus to resume the farming they had learned from the local Pueblos. For, unlike the Apache, they had adapted their lifestyle when they came south, tending corn and sheep, and becoming master weavers. When the silver boom started they evolved their own superlative jewelry, using the turquoise they had always valued.

Navajo have always been quick to absorb new skills, shaping them to fit their own traditions, as they have been quick to comprehend exploitation and to resist it or turn it to their own advantage. When uranium was discovered on their land they did not hope to defend themselves with noble speeches; they hired good land lawyers. When Monument Valley became popular as a backdrop to westerns, they soon learned the going rate for location hire and demanded that film Indians should be Navajo, not white. When tourists resented paying a fair price for handmade jewelry they were provided with cheaper varieties manufactured from reconstituted stones. What I found amusing about this was the indignation with which it was reported, as if it were unreasonable, not to say corrupt, for Indians to refuse to allow themselves to be fleeced, let alone do a little mild fleecing themselves. Good Indians should be sober, photogenic, industrious, and, preferably, unpaid.

We loped along easily for a while before glimpsing the road and heading for it, for the map said "Pump Wash": whatever that meant, it sounded watery.

A pickup was stopped by the roadside; a man, woman, and girl were watching us. Slightly apprehensive, we rode toward them.

"Hi!" cried the man. "How're you doin'?"

"Great," we said, admired the country, and asked about water at the pump.

"Sure there's water, but wouldn't beer be better?" He reached in the icebox for a cold couple. "How much you want for that horse?" He was well oiled, and cheerful. I gave his little girl a ride on Rosie, who did not want to leave Duchess. "Good horse," he said, "but I guess you're okay, too," throwing his arms around Duchess's neck.

"Er—she's nervous of strangers," we warned him.

"She knows I don't mean harm," he said, pawing at her face in a way that generally offends horses. "Horses can see your spirit: they know when there's bad in there." Duchess, usually poised for flight at the proximity of a strange man, curled herself around him like a purring kitten.

Rick told him we were going to Hopi, and asked about fences.

"Ain't no fences," he said, leaning on Duchess and waving his beer can northward. "All Navajo tribal lands, to the mesas."

"I thought it was Hopi for the last twenty miles."

The Hopi reservation is an island in Navajoland. For the last few years its borders, ill-defined by the original settlement, had been under legal dispute. Although they occupy identical territory, the two tribes have different lifestyles: Navajo, traditionally nomadic, now live in separate family homesteads, farming the communal land around them, while Hopi have always lived on top of each other in pueblo villages, traveling out to their crops and herds. Seeing these apparently untended, the Navajo had helped themselves to both, and tried to settle the land. The Hopi, finally waking up to the fact that peaceful reasoning would not stop them, had called in the tribal councils and the law.

The woman spoke up: "No, it's ours now. They don't use it: why should it be theirs? We'll take it from them." They both laughed. "We need more land: Navajo are growing stronger."

We finished our beer, and returned the cans. "Sorry, I don't like throwing them down," Rick said.

"No," agreed the man, and planted them in a little cluster in the sand. "We'll leave them here as a memorial to mark our meeting at this spot."

Pump Wash was a strip of sand in a dry gulch. An outsized pump handle stood above a long metal trough. It took a while to raise water, and when it came it was cool and clear, but Duchess did not like it. We left the horses to pick what herbage they could and climbed the side of the gulch. From the top of a rise we could see the land falling all the way down to the dirty smudge of Winslow, while ahead it was a sea of clear gold where thin dry grass replaced the sagebrush. Volcanic spikes, flat-topped buttes and mesas rose like chocolate-brown islands from a rolling ocean. Above, higher than the buzzards, wheeled an eagle, but I lost him against the sun.

Rolling dust-balls whizzed into the wash, resolving themselves into two pickups full of water barrels. Most homes hereabouts have no water supply. We lay and watched from half a mile away as tiny figures struggled to replenish the barrels. Then they examined our horses, bent over our gear, looked around without spotting us, and went away. I felt like hollering the news down to Winslow.

Beyond the wash were the first houses, scattered miles apart on the plain. Typically each compound held a small, simple house, a privy, a traditional eight-sided hogan made of logs or railroad ties, a shed, and perhaps a small tepee in which ceremonies are held. They were impeccably neat: the contrast to the squalor surrounding the trailer homes around Paulden could not have been more stark. Though winter must be hard in that high, treeless land, and summer baking, it was idyllic in the cool autumn sunshine, a place where your children could grow up in safety among neighbors you knew, where the grandeur of the landscape and the clarity of the air engender serenity. We loped along for hours, finally picking up a dirt track that wound south of twin spires and led us to Felix and Susie's at dusk.

We sat in the kitchen, chattering. Susie, slimmer and more vivacious than most Navajo women, questioned us eagerly about our living conditions at home, surprised to find that we, too, had no electricity or water. We hastened to explain that it is unusual, and that in Wales water is never far away. The idea of it pouring down hillsides overhung with fern and moss, so much of it that you cannot even distinguish its smell, made her fine dark eyes brilliant with wonder; the idea of it raining for a month or two nonstop made her pretty daughter giggle with disbelief. It was hard explaining about drizzle and mud.

Felix returned a couple of hours later. He is a roping champion and had been at the weeklong rodeo in Gallup, New Mexico, winning yet another prize belt buckle. He was an impressive man, handsome and square-jawed, his power and sureness tempered by gentleness. He sat down and attacked his chin with a pair of tweezers, plucking out a couple of hairs.

"Indian no hair on face," he grunted in a parody of film Indians. "Hair on top, hair down below, that's all you need. You guys don't know where to stop."

"Sounds pretty typical," Rick said.

"Well, you said that."

After supper we talked for hours, smoking Indian tobacco, which Felix rolled in maize leaves, passing it around like a joint. Whether it was mildly intoxicating, or whether the soft colors of the rugs, the homely simplicity of the room, the harmony of our conversation on what matters in life, and the feeling of privilege in being invited to share produced the sensation of ease and relaxation, I do not know; but it was an evening of peace that seemed to extend far beyond the walls of the house, linking us to the wet woods waiting in another land.

Susie was kneading dough.

"Like fry-bread?"

"Um, yes," I lied, or thought I did. But Susie's fry-bread was not slices of Wonder Bread oozing in fat: it was a wondrous dry puff produced by deep-frying the light dough. Ten-year-old Miranda sucked jam off her fingers and studied us, in a dither. She had barely plucked up courage to speak to us, yet she had been allocated the task of guiding us on the twenty-mile ride to the school. When we saw the horse that Felix led out for her we understood her misgivings. It was his rodeo mare, a huge charger, monstrously muscled, dancing about looking for a cow to attack. Miranda wept and tried to hide in Susie, but Felix picked her up, threw her on the mare, gave her the reins, and slapped the horse on the rump.

"Oh, Felix, no!" cried Susie, but it was too late. Miranda hurtled away, yipping in terror, until we managed to overhaul her and slew our horses around in front of hers. Tears rolled down her face.

"I don't want to!"

"It's okay, we're not going to make you do anything you don't want. Would you rather ride my horse? She's gentle."

She shook her head mournfully, then wiped her face with one hand, clutching the reins with the other. "No, he said to ride this one." The mare was still galloping, on the spot, straining at the bit.

"All right. Now, just relax your legs, you're gripping so hard she wants to run. There. Now give her a bit of rein so she walks . . . and lean back and stop." I made her practice stopping until she knew she could, Rick assuring her I was the most trustworthy teacher in the world, until she allowed the mare to tiptoe forward uneasily. After an hour we had covered maybe a mile, in shifty shuffle reminiscent of Modestine's pace, "as much slower than a walk as a walk is than a run." Twenty miles: a twenty-hour ride? But as we crept into a bit of badland, eroded humps of striped gravel at the base of the twin spires, she cheered up, laughing at our attempts to reproduce the varieties of Navajo glottal stop, and even daring to brave a few steps of a jog.

The badlands mocked us. The washes turned back on themselves, and the tops turned into precipices. There was no chance of getting to the school for lunch, as Felix had estimated; nor could we get rid of the piebald sheepdog that followed us. As we scrambled through the precipitous ra-vines between the spires and padded across the waterless plain his tongue lolled longer and longer, and he refused to budge from the poor shade holes he dug in the sand. Miranda seemed not to worry about him, but I did not want to abandon him, for it seemed unlikely he would survive. I had to ride at him to make him move.

We rounded a butte to see, in the distance, a grove of cottonwoods by a water tower.

"There's the school!" Miranda cried, flinging out her right hand. Unfortunately she was also pointing at a distant cow. The mare shot forward, intent upon its prey, while I thundered behind shouting instructions. They slid to a halt in a whirl of dust. She was bent over the saddle horn, shaking.

"I shouldn't have done that." She was giggling, not crying.

"You're a brave girl."

She straightened up with a wicked grin. "I've missed a whole day of class! But there's racing, too; I don't want to miss that."

There was a scattering of low buildings under shade trees, and Felix with a hose of cool water, dunking the dog. He seemed more impressed by its achievement than his daughter's: he had had no doubts about her. We went to watch the racing, a long cross-country over hilly desert. The Hopi juniors had arrived in buses. They were noticeably more delicate than the robust, broad-faced Navajo children, but are renowned for their stamina as runners. A crowd of children, most of them barefoot, sped away in a cloud of dust.

Gordon watched his protégés anxiously. He had designed the course carefully, incorporating a long hill intended to wear out the unsuspecting visitors who did not know how to pace themselves.

"We like to encourage these competitions," he said. "The achievement gives them something to be proud of, success to be worked for."

But when the candy-bar prizes were given out, Felix murmured: "These guys will never learn. They think the kids will value prizes, but they just go around the corner and share them with everybody else. Our children are taught not to push themselves forward or think themselves better than others: we teach them to share, to help one another."

The effect was striking. Having taught in summer camps, I was used to the brash eagerness of American children shouting "Me, me, me." These children were as interested and lively as any healthy youngsters, but seemed almost intuitively well mannered, treating each other and us with gentle courtesy. There were no playground squabbles, but their toughness and courage were apparent: in a fast game of basketball they shrugged off injury without a moment's hesitation, oblivious to blood and bruises. They greeted us with the hand sign for "peace" and huddled around to hear our stories, stroking our knees.

Many of them live in such remote places that from the age of five or six they sleep at the school. At one time it was government policy to take all Indian children from their families and put them in boarding schools, the better to inculcate Christianity and American values in them; but more recently respect for their different culture has led to less repressive attitudes. The older classes were taught mainly by whites, but the rest of the staff was Navajo. After school, Susie sat among a crowd of children making Halloween decorations and telling them of skinwalkers, the Navajo version of witches in wolves' clothing. She insisted she had glimpsed one, shaggy and swift, in the headlights of the truck one night. I asked Felix for a coyote story, but he said that, like playing with string, they were only for winter.

I slept in a bunk bed in the girls' dormitory, among a crowd of shining black heads.

What they made of our "teaching" I do not know. The similarity between these children and the shy, polite children from our hill farms—their bilingualism, relative poverty and unemployment, Anglo attitudes toward the language and culture of subject races—these made for striking parallels that were as difficult to skirt around as to discuss delicately. Later, they led a vigorous exchange of correspondence and drawings between this school and our tiny local primary school.

We went from class to class discussing rain and sheep. The younger children invariably asked us our clans. When we said we had none, it was as if we said we had no gender, an impossible concept. Encouraged by their facility with strange sounds, we taught the eight-year-olds to sing "*Sospan Fach,*" surely a Historic Event. Echoes of Cardiff Arms Park in high trebles wafted over the desert.

A ball of fire roared twenty feet into the night sky, and the children gasped. Rick spun and chanted, licked flame, wove a web of it around himself. He toyed with it, caressed his bare skin with it, swallowed and regurgitated it, and when he had worked himself up into a passion, blew out another rumbling roll of flame. In the brief illumination the children's eyes were round with delight. Again and again the dragon's breath roared; and then there was nothing but darkness, silence, and the chill wind of the desert.

Even in the middle of nowhere, with the wrong equipment, Rick is an artist with fire. Self-consciousness thrown to the wind, he makes love to it, rejoicing in his facility with it like a seal playing in water. His kisses taste horrible for days.

I was afraid, at first, of seeming intrusive, a tourist grabbing at souvenirs of experience; afraid, too, that the romantic notions I had for so long entertained would distort my perceptions and attempts to communicate. But the women put me at ease with their openness and warmth. Women who devote themselves to nurturing small children, either their own or others', often seem less bewildered than men by challenges to their traditional culture; for they can at least be certain that their role and responsibilities do not lie in wondering whether or how to prove their worth in a society whose values are volatile and often conflicting, but outside themselves, in raising healthy, secure children. There is ground under their feet, whatever turmoil the winds of change might be wreaking above. The lullabies that comforted them comfort their children too.

These women were as solid as oaks, playful in their solemnity, accepting me like a long-lost sister. Without hesitation we delved into topics I would usually not broach with strangers for fear of embarrassing them, though the readiness with which they extended and developed our discussions showed that they were not only accustomed to them, but more practiced in ways of thinking about them.

So it was that when Karen, who drove the minibus, asked one day if I would like to come on the long drive to deliver the day children home, we found ourselves talking about what her pregnancy and the birth of her son, whom I was to meet later, frizz-headed and thoughtful on his cradle-board, had meant to her. She spoke so clearly about her feelings that I found I could, without rancor or feeling like a bad omen, talk about my baby too, and feel again the joy I had felt in carrying him. And in the calmness with which she accepted my tale, the lack of protestation or overeager sympathy, her understanding that the similarity of our feelings drew us together more than the difference in our fortunes separated us, came at last a sense, made possible by the stark clarity of that elemental land, of resolution in the recognition that the joy had had nothing to do with expectation, nor with the grief that followed. It was a thing in itself, that he had given me forever.

Understanding for the first time the independence of these emotions, it became clear that I could shuck off the shell of pain that had so enclosed and confused matters, and leave it in the dust with no feeling of abandoning or betraying him, but only gratitude.

I was silent as all this unfolded within me, but she knew. She stopped the van suddenly, and we gazed out together.

"You are all right now, though," she said gently, after a while.

"Yes. It is this land, and you people."

"You came here."

"I didn't know." Or did I? Was there some white light in the back of my mind that was guiding me in what seemed to be mere blind thrashing about?

Feeling rather foolish, I told her of my childhood fancies, of that photograph of Chelly. "But I've always felt that it would be artificial to try to immerse myself in your beliefs in the hope of gaining the understanding that they bring you. I wasn't brought up in your tradition: that knowledge could only be superficial, not part of me. Unfortunately I find the Christian tradition I was taught singularly lacking in spiritual value."

"Yes, that's true. Then you must let your spirit find your own way. So you came here. What you recognized and felt was real, you know. This—" waving her hand over the golden plain "—is truly a part of your spirit, and your spirit knew it immediately."

It was in that land of my spirit that the pain of unacceptable reality left me, and I left my child. He is buried on a Welsh hillside; but it is there, between the dust and the eagles, that I think of him as being at peace.

Another release, another unfolding, in that great outer circuit where clarity is gained. But the final laps of the journey remained. The cliffs of the Hopi mesas beckoned.

The going was soft and easy underfoot, which was just as well, since Rosie had lost a shoe. But even without the packs, which Gordon and Rick had ferried to Hopi, it was bound to be a long day. Excitement mingled with apprehension. I was still reeling slightly from the last round, feeling the balance of my psyche revised in a way to which I was not yet accustomed. An insect emerging from the outgrown shell of its last molt pats its soft new shape as if wondering how it will behave. People who knew the Hopi spoke and wrote of them with such reverence, awe almost, that I feared I would still prove blundering and inadequate.

I do not know what we expected, except to find the maze that was, to an extent that we had not yet realized, the totem of this journey; but we were expecting something, even if only to be found wanting. But this apprehension could not dispel my delight that, like the land, we were rising, indeed had risen and were aloft, cruising easily. We were in good shape, the horses shining and fit, their problems and naiveté overcome;

our minimal equipment had served us well and we had neither found anything lacking nor, apart from the snakebite kit, surplus; we had become a slick, self-contained operation at last, able to go on forever. We cantered over the gentle land for mile after mile. Beyond Seba Dalkai there were few houses, then none, and no trees; only the dark buttes sliding past disturbed the tranquil swell of leonine land.

I watched Rosie's striped feet sink into the sand, and remembered a Navajo song:

> My horse has hoofs like striped agate,
> His fetlock's like a fine eagle plume.
> His legs are like quick lightning.
> My horse's body is an eagle-plumed arrow.
> My horse's tail is a trailing black cloud.
>
> His mane is made of short rainbows.
> My horse's ears are made of round corn.
> My horse's eyes are big stars.
> My horse's head is made of mixed waters
>   from the holy streams. He never knows
>   thirst.
> My horse's teeth are of white shell.
> In his mouth, for a bridle, is a long rainbow
> With which I guide him.

Tiny dots far away suddenly boiled into action, and one shot like an eagle-plumed arrow toward us, trailing a dust cloud. His neigh was the unmistakable cry of a stallion in pursuit of fresh mates. We wheeled the mares and galloped hard, but he was gaining on us fast, when, like a life jacket to a drowning man, a fence appeared. We hammered along it, searching for an openable bit, found one, and scrabbled through it with the stallion literally on our heels. Rick galloped back along our side of it to distract him while I tried to close it with shaking hands.

The fence looked none too stock-proof, and we galloped away down a long slope to get clear. I thought we were doing well until I realized we were in a two-horse stampede, completely unable to stop. Duchess sailed past me like Secretariat, effortless, huge-striding, Rick riding the majestic rolls of her power with a smile of bemused wonder. They flew onward. But after a couple of miles the slope plunged downward, growing rockier. Every time we tried to pull them up, the bitches bucked and squealed. We hurtled downhill, leaping headlong over rocks and scrub in a narrow wash, and forced them up the other side until they ran out of breath. They turned and snorted furiously at the angry dot now miles away. When we headed on, the cliffs had grown much larger.

The Hopi mesas stretch southward like the stubby digits of a three-fingered hand laid upon a high plateau. On each of the fingernails is a village: Oraibi, the oldest continuously inhabited site in North America, on the third, westernmost mesa; Shongolovi on the second, with Shipaulovi, our final destination, on its knuckle; and Walpi, where they walk on fire, on the first. As Second Mesa loomed larger, we could begin to make out the stone houses, almost indistinguishable from the crumbling cliff on which they perched, and the scattering of newer houses at the bottom of the cliff. But when night fell, bringing a bitter wind from the top of the mesa, we were still far away.

Rick has trouble with heat, I with cold. As we stumbled along in the dark, all the clothes we had could not protect me from the incessant wind that rattled through my bones. We came into an area of corn; the low plants grew straight from dry dust, clattering icily against the horses' legs. My body seemed to reach absolute zero, that depth of cold where even molecular vibration stops. Even walking did not help, for my limbs ceased to function properly. I was ashamed at letting Rick down: he had so longed to be here, and this rigid wreck was no fit companion for a triumphant arrival. Coyote was stalking us, teeth in my Achilles' heel.

He had the last laugh, of course. The final circuit is never easy.

Late at night we swung onto the road, found the houses at the bottom of the cliff, and went around to the haybarn where we were to camp. Even the protection of a stack of alfalfa did not raise the temperature. I saw to Rosie, dragged out a sleeping bag, and lay in a frozen huddle, too cold even to shiver, while Rick heroically put up the tent, made a fire, tea, and food, and finally came to warm me. Stars glittered frostily over the mesa.

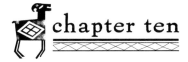

chapter ten

THERE ARE ABOUT six thousand Hopi—more, perhaps, than there were when the Spaniards looking for the fabulous seven cities of gold first came across them. According to their history they did not migrate southward from the Bering Straits crossing, like other Indians, but island-hopped across the Pacific from the west to Central America when they emerged after the Flood: the islands, they say, sank back into the ocean. On landing, the various clans migrated in different directions, each evolving its own traditions and particular concerns, sometimes splitting into subclans, sometimes settling too long and becoming lost. There are now some forty clans, whose migrations led them to the limits of both Americas, the Atlantic, the Pacific, the frozen north and even Tierra del Fuego before spiraling slowly back to the spiritual center of the world on the mesas.

The stories of what happened to them reflect every facet of human experience: discovery and loss, friendship and treachery, the power of their faith and their weakness without it. They are the struggles of people trying not so much to overcome their environment and their limitations as to see how both fit together in an integrated whole. We are part of this world, not its lords and masters, and we must strive to understand and harmonize with the underlying forces that govern it. Despite its poverty, our spiritual potential is as important a facet of us as our physical well-being, which seems to dominate modern life. For this Fourth World is geared to the basest, the most material, of the psychophysical centers corresponding to the Eastern *chakras*. It will be destroyed by holocaust, possibly caused by nuclear war.

The Fifth World that succeeds it will represent, for the first time, an upward step, for it will be inherited by those who have seen where unbridled materialism leads. Indeed, the present and growing ecological awareness foreshadows the coming change, as perhaps does the buildup of nuclear arms in unstable nations still greedy for power and "progress." These beliefs, dating from a time long before the Hopi had met white men (one of whom is to be a kind of Messiah) and far before the discovery of atomic weapons, were unknown to Rick and me when we started on our journey: we found them in Frank Waters's *Book of the Hopi*, which seemed to indicate the aptness of the path we were taking, and they were confirmed again and again in discussions.

The *Book of the Hopi* also describes the numerous ceremonies, some of which are almost theatrical events lasting many days, for which the Hopi are famed. These ceremonies, in which the knowledge held by different clans interlinks, form an integrated representation of the cycle of the earth and its part in creation. They are full of detailed symbolism, including people impersonating kachinas, the spirits who represent creation's underlying principles. Parts of some of these ceremonies are open to tourists, but we had no particular desire to see them without being able to contribute at least some understanding, feeling that the spiritual force generated by believers is dissipated by those who come only to take. I hate cathedrals full of camera clicks and chatter.

That the ceremonies still exist is a tribute to their power. The Spaniards, of course, sent missionaries to convert the Hopi, fairly forcefully; when the rains failed after the ceremonies were stopped, and recovered after they were performed in secret, the Hopi determined to rid themselves of missionaries. Together with all the other Pueblos in Arizona and New Mexico, they plotted to kill them all on the same night, August 10, 1680, sack the missions, and drive the Spaniards back to Mexico.

After the Pueblo Revolt the Spaniards trod less arrogantly. They were not interested in conquest but in riches, of which the Hopi had few. Nevertheless, they still managed to convert a large number of Hopi in the village of Awatovi. This the Hopi destroyed, massacring their own people in their determination to hold fast to what they believed preserved the natural order of the world. For the People of Peace, dedicated to harmony, it was an act as appalling as it was desperate, undermining their faith as well as underpinning it.

The Anglos who arrived after the Spaniards left them alone, seeing nothing of value or threat in the shambling clifftop shacks, the barren land. The Hopi even swore allegiance to the United States government in exchange for a promise to protect them against the depredations of the Navajo, who had by then arrived in force and were busy appropriating their herds and land as well as their skills and beliefs. Naturally it was not a promise the government upheld, but compared with the way that other Indians were treated, the Hopi got off lightly. They kept themselves to themselves, in peace.

The Hopi have never pretended to be perfect, nor to hold the One True Faith. They try to work together but, human nature being what it is, they sometimes fail. They have done better than most. Despite clan squabbles, despite Awatovi even, despite the invasion of the twentieth century, they are still trying to hold the world together the way it should be.

Rosy light caught the houses on the clifftops and spilled down the shattered crags. I was so excited to be there, after what had seemed such impossibilities, that *joie de vivre* drove me out onto the freezing sand to scrabble for sagebrush roots and make a fire. The shadow crept downward like an ebbing tide, exposing the rock rearing above us to pink-gold splendor. I waited until the light surrounded our barn before greeting Rick with a cup of tea. It was time to celebrate.

"Rick, my love, look."

"Uh."

"Look, look: it's brilliant."

He did not move. Ah well, I thought, he's often slow to wake, and he did put in all the effort last night. I went for a stroll up the wash. The cliffs and villages were scrappy and, once the rosiness had left the light, the rock was drab. Around us, at the base of the cliffs, were a few modern houses and untidy pens. It was not a place of great beauty, though the elevation, the warmth of the sun radiating through the cold air, and the excitement of a desert dawn were exhilarating.

The fire had gone out, and his tea was cold. I made more.

"Rick, do get up, it's—"

"Can't."

"What do you mean, can't?"

He said slowly: "Hurts. Like hell. Can't move."

The altitude? That savage cold last night? His heroic kindness when he was exhausted?

"Be all right in a while," he said; but he did not reach for his essential first cigarette.

By midmorning it was obviously not merely the result of a hard night. He really could not move, and felt barely alive to the touch. He had a terrible constricting pain centered, he finally confessed, around his heart, so awful that he could barely breathe. I know little about hearts, but I thought that if they hurt for that long you were dead, and though he huddled in a miserable heap as if pole-axed, he was not going colder. His lungs, rotted from years of smoking? Perhaps it was the alfalfa? Some people react badly to it.

I moved him out into the sunshine, away from the barn. He could barely walk. But even hours later he was no better. I started to worry. What on earth were the medical facilities if he needed a doctor? Should I try to hitch him a lift to the hospital in Flagstaff? I remembered that our insurance had just run out . . . He kept insisting he would be all right, and saying, why didn't I go and explore. I hated to leave him, but by late afternoon the frustration of doing nothing overcame me, and he was just the same. I decided to throw myself on the mercies of the Hopi. Rosie was still shoeless; I saddled the Duchess.

We trotted down the road along the bottom of the mesa toward the finger on which Shongolovi perches. A convoy of tourists in camper-vans overtook us, slowing down to choke us in smelly fumes and lean out of the window for snapshots; some even stopped, the better to focus, but not to say hello or thank you. By the time we were halfway up the steep hairpins to the village I was furious at their rudeness. At the top, the mesa was truly table-flat and the view over the land we had traveled stupendous. The plateau spread in softly mottled umbers and ochers, the buttes and spires rising solid from the heat haze. I tried to work out which were the ones by the school, and Felix's twin spires; with a telescope I might even have picked out the black tank from the dark strip of range on the horizon. What would it be like to live in this close huddle of little houses with that vision of immensity constantly to remind you of your place in the scheme of things? Duchess and I gazed. She was a horse with a love of great spaces.

"Hi," said a young man sitting in a car. "Can I take your picture?"

I burst out laughing. "You, of all people?" Behind me was a sign at the entrance to the village: NO PHOTOGRAPHS. NO VIDEOS. LEAVE ALL RECORDING EQUIPMENT IN YOUR CAR.

He laughed, too. "I'm the official photographer." We introduced ourselves.

"Official?"

"I take photographs of all our artifacts, all the petroglyphs, so we can catalog them before they disappear."

"Why are they disappearing?"

"The tourists take them for souvenirs."

I could imagine them, rapacious as herring gulls tearing at a carcass. The carvings represent the Hopi's historical record: the clans, their migrations, their beliefs, in symbols whose full meaning only a Hopi could possibly understand. I felt ashamed of being white. But were we any better? I explained about our pilgrimage and our quest. He seemed to find it entirely fitting.

"There are a couple of square mazes on the rocks down there," he said, pointing, "but the one I think you mean is along there." He indicated Shipaulovi, the village below which we were camped, farther along the mesa. "You can take the way along the top of the cliffs."

He took our photo under the sign.

I did not want to look for the maze without Rick, but I could at least avoid the road by going along the top . . .

The dirt track led across slabs of bare sandstone where Duchess's feet skidded and clattered; it divided again and again, and the branches I took brought us to a handful of little houses hidden among juniper bushes. Children ran out and waved; dogs barked; a man came out.

"I'm sorry," I said. "I didn't mean to intrude; maybe I've got the wrong track."

He sat on the hood of his pickup shelling pistachios, and we talked. He was gentle and friendly, with an open, direct gaze. I said I was upset at hearing of the tourists' behavior.

"They are lost," he said. "Their lives have no meaning, so they try to steal it. But these souvenirs do not make their spirits rich." He did not sound condemnatory, but saddened. He said: "Christianity is a problem. It is the teaching that you are born into sin." I saw again a christening of a friend's baby, remembering my intuitive revulsion at the priest's pronouncement that the offended infant wriggling in his arms was by nature unclean, and must spend her life in a prolonged and guilty struggle against herself. "But people are not evil in themselves. When we lose our way we may do bad things, but that does not make us bad. When you think you are bad, as you are taught, you want material things to make you feel less uncomfortable."

I told him of Samuel Baker, who explored the upper reaches of the Nile, writing: "Christianity cannot exist apart from civilization; thus, the spread of Christianity must depend upon the extension of civilization; and that civilization depends upon commerce . . . The savage must learn to *want*, he must learn to be ambitious; and to covet more than the mere animal necessities of food and drink." (Or, as Senator Dawes, who conceived the idea of forcing Indians to give up their communal land ownership in favor of allotments, said: "There is no selfishness, which is at the bottom of civilization.")

"I'm not sure I approve of this civilization," I said.

"Well, I'm a savage," he said grinning.

We talked of modern materialism, of the split within the Hopi between the traditionalists who refuse any change in their way of life and the progressives who believe that some compromise is necessary. As we talked, I was seized with the conviction that I must tell this man about Rick.

"He's sick, but I can't help feeling that there's more to it than that, something to do with having got here at last. He so wanted to be here, but his body has gone on strike." I told him of our difficulties on the way, of Rick's attitudes and ideals, of what we had learned. "I'm sorry, it's not your concern . . ."

He was looking at me thoughtfully with that unblinking gaze. My heart started thumping: I felt naked. He glanced at his wife, who had come to join us. She nodded almost imperceptibly. He gave, with a smile, the reason that my path had led to his door:

"My father's the medicine man."

I rode off along the top of the mesa wondering what Rick would think about seeing a medicine man, wondering if he would think that the terrible inner flaws that he believes he has (perhaps he understood the priest who christened him) would be revealed in some soul-shaking manner. Yet I knew that these people, warm and direct, would only help him, and anyway he had nothing to fear.

Duchess, to whom I had been paying little attention as we jogged along, for my head was full of Rick, stopped suddenly beside a large boulder and stared at it intently. Horses do sometimes react strongly to rocks, especially ones about the size of a pig, or maybe a camouflaged lion; but this was much bigger, with nothing remarkable about it. Perhaps she was just tired of being an unconsulted vehicle. Douglas Adams says: "They have always understood a great deal more than they let on. It is difficult to be sat on all day, every day, by some other creature, without forming an opinion about them. On the other hand, it is perfectly possible to sit all day, every day, on top of another creature and not have the slightest thought about them whatsoever."

I laughed and stroked her back, turning to look again at that immensity of land, orange now in the evening sun, thinking of her early terrors and their gradual dissipation, and marveling yet again at the closeness we can achieve with horses. The Indians who met early Spanish invaders thought that horse and man were one animal, so closely do the two fuse when they have traveled so many miles and endured so many vicissitudes together. In Duchess I could feel Rick, and having drunk in the peace of the vista, could feel that his problems, too, would be solved. Optimism overcame me: as we skidded down the steep road from Shipaulovi I had even convinced myself he was better already.

He was not. He looked terrible, his tanned face like an old brown skull. Pain had exhausted him. I told him about the medicine man. "He's in his fields, only a couple of miles away."

"I don't think I can get there."

"Tomorrow morning. We'll go slow. Duchess is smooth. If you'd spoken to his son, you'd know."

When I crawled in beside him, his body felt lifeless.

Dawn. The pale shifting colors, ancient as the earth, unfolded in the biting cold. The golden crescent slung its rays of life and hope at me, but Rick lay like a corpse. Was I being irresponsible? Foolishly romantic? I got up to make smoky tea.

It was hard getting him into the saddle; hard, too, to watch his pain. We could not go the easiest way, for there was a burial ground we should not cross, so we headed directly across the plain. Water running from the mesas had eroded gullies we had to scramble up and down; he groaned when Duchess skipped or twisted. We found a dirt track, which was easier, but two miles turned into two hours. The sun climbed the sky, and there was nothing but bleached range. I should have known. People who have always lived in the same place find even the concept of giving directions almost impossible. I felt horribly guilty for his pain on what might turn out to be a wild-goose chase: there was nothing out there but the breeze and the dust as far as we could see.

Another hour slid by before we spotted a tiny white trailer. Beside it, a patch of combed-looking dust turned into rows of sparse, desiccated corn. A man crawled among them. Rick slithered off Duchess and collapsed. I went over to the man.

"Your son said you might help us. My friend is sick."

"Never mind, I fix him," he said cheerfully. Anybody less like my vision of a solemn, portentous medicine man could not be imagined. He was merry, frisky, and rotund; brown eyes with a gaze as direct as his son's twinkled in his round face. "I fix him. You help me with the corn."

"Thank you."

"He's your husband?" he asked as we went toward Rick.

"No, but I love him."

He gave me a beaming smile. "Okay, I fix him."

Rick had struggled upright. The man said: "You sick, huh? You're sick. Never mind." He ran his hands down Rick's chest. Immediately, he said: "This side not working." He patted Rick's left side. "Nothing working. All stopped. Never mind, I fix him. Kneel down."

Rick knelt in the dust beside the corn. The man stood behind him, patting his back; then he put his arms around Rick's chest, clasped his right hand around the back of Rick's neck, and wrenched sharply. Rick groaned.

"I fix," the man cried happily, hitting him smartly. He pummeled and wrenched, slapped and thumped, asking Rick to cough from time to time. "There, better, eh?"

"I don't know," Rick said miserably.

From his pocket the man took, I think, a stone, which he kept concealed in his hand, and passed it up and down Rick's back, thumping him occasionally. Then he passed his hands thoughtfully up and down, and pronounced Rick cured.

"Maybe," Rick said, breathing heavily. "Maybe."

"How you do this?"

"I didn't do anything. I just went to bed okay and woke up like this. I did get dumped off my horse a couple of months ago, but I've been fine since then."

"You work 'round horses, maybe you swallow a fly."

"I don't think so."

"Yes, you swallow a fly. Now I take him out. Open your mouth. No, to the sky." He peered in. "Yes, there he is."

I do not think that any of us believed in that fly, but I watched him pick a stem of dry grass, fish into Rick's mouth with it, and draw out something as tangible as it was invisible. He drew it out with infinite care, lest it drop off the straw, cupped his other hand around it, took a few steps back, and threw it away with a frown.

"Okay, you better now. Now we pick corn." He slapped Rick's back cheerfully. "Strong young man, good for work."

Rick looked shell-shocked.

"Do you feel any better?" I asked as we made our way up the rows of corn. He looked worse.

"Sore. Ten rounds with Muhammad Ali," he mumbled. "God, I hurt."

Hopi corn is unlike any other. It is an ancient strain, adapted for the desert. It is planted a foot or so deep, so that it does not germinate unless the ground has been sufficiently soaked to ensure its survival until fruition. It is too precious to waste. It grows only a couple of feet high; by harvesting time it is brown and lifeless, an untidy bundle of broad leaves concealing its treasure. The kernels on the cobs are blue: dark, rich, lustrous blue, or sometimes maroon, or even a mosaic of colors. They are not soft and juicy, but hard and dry.

Blue corn is sacred, for it gives us life. With its male tassel above and female flower below, it embodies the dichotomy that, united, brings forth fruit. Kokopelli, the

Kokopilav

dancing flute player, carried its seeds, along with those of other plants, in the hump on his back as he skipped across continents clothing them with vegetation and warmth from the music of his flute. A perfect ear of corn, or fine-ground flour, is used in many ceremonies. Only the women may grind it: a Hopi girl is taught how after she first menstruates, investing this transition from girlhood to young womanhood with clarity and dignity instead of the confused secrecy that we undergo. She is also taught to make *piki*, using a smooth flat stone that has been handed down her female line for generations. After heating it in a fire, she brushes it swiftly with fingers dipped in a thin batter made with corn meal and the water from bean ash. The crisp sheets, thinner than paper, that result are rolled up around each other to make a many-layered bun, light and flaky as puff pastry, and bright blue. It is an extraordinary skill.

We went down the rows of corn joking with the medicine man, plucking these remarkable cobs until we had several boxes full. Despite his pummeling Rick seemed to be moving more easily.

"Will he be all right?" I asked anxiously.

"Oh, yes. But he was really very sick. There are other

things you must do for him." He explained. "You will do that, won't you? It is important."

"Of course. It is very kind of you to help us."

"I help you, you help me." How could I say that this felt more like a privilege than work? "I fix many people, whites too. Once I fixed a man who came from California: he had bad cancer, too bad to cut it out, and they said he would die, but I gave him medicine and it went away. His doctors said they could not understand it. It was hard even for me to do, but I know all the plants."

"I met a man who said there were no plants good for healing here," I teased.

"No, no," he cried excitedly. "They all have their powers, but you must know which ones are good for what, and how to use them. Everything has its place; it all fits together."

"Even this?" I indicated the cockleburs invading the corn patch. "They're not quite in the right place."

"Not for my corn, maybe, but when you have trouble here—" he pointed to the front of his trousers "—then this is very good, this one. Come, now we eat."

We went to the trailer and sat outside in the sun. His wife was shelling beans, beautiful mottled purple beans enclosed in blackened pods. She had baskets of other types, too, in strange colors and shapes; but we picnicked on supermarket bread and cheese. Sheep wandered off the range to invade the corn patch, to his dismay. I jumped on Rosie bareback and chased them out. Seeing how handy she was, he wanted to buy her, but I said she was spoken for; nevertheless he was intrigued by the fact that I rode her, always had ridden her, in a halter, and wanted to try her out. I saddled her up but she did not want to go far from me, to my embarrassment; but by then his attention had switched to my saddle, a Canadian cavalry saddle I had bought in Chino Valley. It had been ridden by a cowboy who sat farther back than I do, so it was uncomfortable for me; but he loved it, liking, too, its light weight compared with that of a western saddle. We pulled it off and discussed it, but I found him fondling my bottom appreciatively.

"This is very good," he said, squeezing me; "round and firm. Hopi girls are too broad and flat here. Why don't you stay in Hopi, so we can breed girls with fine fannies?"

When we rode home Rick was still in pain, though he said it did not feel so constricting. We called round to our hosts' house to give them a belated greeting and explain about Rick's collapse. Honani, whose name means badger, was clearly a progressive, owning a fine gift shop in the village. Appropriately he produced some strong painkillers: Badger clan are traditionally occupied with healing and help. I played hide-and-seek with his little boy, a lively toddler who was fascinated by my long sun-bleached hair; his wife watched with apprehension, then amusement when I assured her I enjoyed his playfulness.

I failed to keep a journal while we were in Hopi. Neither of us can remember the sequence of events, nor even how long we were there, though the impressions themselves are as clear as the desert air. Hopi seemed to have its own time, its own logic, at once unfathomable and immediate. We seemed to live as if in a dream, with little conscious control over events that included us in their unfolding. Whenever we set out to do something, our projects slithered from our grasp, to be replaced by something unimagined yet often more apposite. In the tightknit, scruffy villages and dingy cliffs there was little to delight the eye, but in the limitless span of the vista, the presence of people free from personal ambition and fear, and their unfussy warmth, there was a wonderful sense of peace and truth.

As we rode down from Shipaulovi, where we had failed to find the man who could tell us more about the maze, two children ran barefoot down the cliff, leaping like goats down the boulders: "Mister, mister, are you the man that eats fire?"

In the supermarket at the bottom of the mesa huge posters advertised the arrival of videos of *Dances With Wolves*.

We went to Honani's shop. It was classy and expensive, selling exquisite silver jewelry engraved with badgers' claws and other symbols, and kachina dolls. These dolls, made from soft cottonwood, are intricately carved and painted, and are used to teach children the different kachinas. In the office, two sophisticated young women were dealing with export trade, checking information on computers as the fax machine poured out demands from Germany. They were interested in Rick's involvement with the maze, and the fact that it was found in Crete and Scandinavia as well as in Tintagel.

"I can see how the idea could have been carried between those places by seagoing people," Rick said. "But to find it here seems extraordinary."

"Probably it means that the Hopi stopped there. They migrated all over the world, you know, not just the Americas."

"Well, I suppose that if they caught the Gulf Stream from the coast of Mexico they might end up in Tintagel."

"When did it appear in Cornwall?"

"About three and a half thousand years ago."

"Oh, then there is no problem," said the woman, turning back to the printer and reaching for the phone marked International Calls. "People had such power in those times, they could have walked over the Atlantic. They could walk on water."

Apart from a few paranoid-looking tourists, the only people we met who were at all reserved were those working in the cultural center, as if too much contact with strangers made them cast a protective curtain of aloofness around themselves. The others were as open and friendly as confident children, hospitable, unselfconscious, and interested in frank, wide-ranging, and often humorous discussions on almost any topic. They seemed far better informed about the rest of the world than most inhabitants of Middle America, though how I do not know. Their material poverty in no way reflected intellectual barrenness.

Riding through Shipaulovi's untidy straggle of small flat-roofed houses, we were greeted by a big man who invited us in to meet his friend, a Havasupai from the reservation at the bottom of the Grand Canyon. He was a firefighter. Many Indians, he said, joined the Fire Service: the job required no particular entrance qualifications, but was an education in itself. An experienced man, as he was, would often be called to fires all over the United States, yet could spend long periods at home with his family and crops. It suited him fine, he said, cheerfully relating hair-raising stories between swigs of Thunderbird.

The big man carved kachina dolls for the gift shops; he showed us a chunk of cottonwood, pale and light as balsa, that he was starting on. Each doll took him a couple of weeks and a good deal of concentration, for he liked to think of the spirit as he worked. I said we had seen a Navajo carving one too.

"Oh, but they only have one kachina to our hundreds," he said, "and even that one they stole from us."

We talked of the tribes' different lifestyles. I said: "If this is anything like Wales, then living in these tight villages must be difficult. Everybody thinks they know everything you do, even when they've got the wrong end of the stick."

He burst out laughing. "Oh, boy, you know, don't you? They never stop gossiping and exchanging tales. They watch you like hawks. You want to bet they all know you're here, and we've got this bottle—here, have some, it's not so bad—and they're all talking? That's why I'm a Christian."

"Why?"

"It's much simpler; not so many things to do and not to do. And God runs the world." Anthropologists say that the Hopi's circumscribed roles and emphasis on responsibility can lead to anxiety and depression. This man's conversion sounded more like an escape than a revelation. There was a small mission near Shipaulovi, though it was not popular, he said. It was on Third Mesa that people adhered most unswervingly to the old ways, refusing electricity or any form of modern living, though apart from a small television his house bore few traces of modernity. If we were interested in tradition, he said, it was a pity we had just missed the Basket Dance, the end of a ceremony that culminated in a giveaway popular with the tourists. He reached for the shoulder blade of a deer on the mantelpiece and showed me how to rub it against the corrugations on a stick to produce a complex, rattling rhythm. I knelt at his feet and played; to his delight I held the rhythm well, and he broke into a long, joyful chant to my accompaniment, clapping and stamping.

We arranged to have breakfast together the next day at an unspecified time, but we failed to turn up early enough because, mysteriously, we had hangovers.

We were crouched by the fire, watching the flames leap in the darkness, and quite suddenly found ourselves surrounded. Four solemn young men, hands behind their backs, were standing over us. They had appeared so silently I almost jumped.

"Hi! How are you doing?"

"We've seen your fires at night." A flat voice, with no hint of intent.

"Yes; we're camping here."

"Mind if we join you?"

I felt relieved, and foolish: what did I expect, from these people? After a few minutes they shyly produced the cans of beer they had been hiding and we talked half the night: of the problems of being a young Hopi male in a matriarchal society ("the women, they have it all their own way") where upon marriage a man joins his wife's mother's household and clan; of the problems of being a Hopi at all in modern America; of music and books and poetry.

One of them was half Hopi, half Navajo, but spoke neither language, which made him feel a total misfit everywhere. He was struggling to express himself in music and poetry, but was too shy to quote any, despite Rick's interest. He, too, writes poetry, and is moreover a walking anthology of poetry he admires, a vast amount of which he knows by heart. He produced a few before we drew the boy out on his own tastes and discovered he had read some extraordinary books, greatly admiring Alice Walker and George Orwell. Where did he come across them? I asked.

He hung his head. "In jail."

There seemed to be no turning back, and we had found Indians ready to discuss anything. So why had he been in jail?

"For hitting a cop. I was drunk."

We both broke out laughing. "Well, if you're running amok you might as well make a good job of it." Now it was they who were relieved; our laughter dissolved the last of their caution about us. He had been in jail a year, reading, thinking, writing: he had, he said, learned far more than he had at the university, which had thrown him out for his misconduct. But where, I thought, could this exuberant intelligence go? They said that most Indians who went to the university dropped out, from sheer bewilderment if not wild living; nothing prepared them for the loudness, the competitive jostle, and the anonymity of American life; and the attitudes to women, and of women, shocked them. Again I could not help being reminded of hill-farm families in Wales, where traditional love of learning has brought about a sophistication of ideas wholly unmatched by practical experience.

They stayed until we were all falling asleep, and one opted to stay all night. In vain we protested he would freeze, but we found an old carpet and he rolled up in that outside our tent. He wanted to hear our traditional songs. "Calon Lan" met with approval, but I could not remember all of "John Barleycorn"; it surprised me to find how many sea songs I knew. In return, he sang me rather monotonous sounding chants that, as I listened, were full of subtle modulations; one of them was the song I had known I was missing, the one I should sing to greet the sun in the morning as I sprinkled blue corn meal in a line to salute him. But in the morning, in the deep purple light of predawn, the carpet was empty, dusted with frost.

Several times we went up to Shongolovi, to report on Rick's recovery and see about the saddle. Mean as it made me feel, I could not afford simply to give the medicine man the saddle: I had to have enough to pay Starr's gas to come and get us. It was less than half what it was worth, and I threw in all the extras I could spare, and the old lady paid with a smile; but I still felt ashamed.

Their hospitality was of easy acceptance, *piki* bread, and warm smiles. The old lady was Sun, one of the last clans to reach the mesas; we had passed the ruins of their last habitation before the mesas near Winslow. Their specialty was the defense of the nation. There was a large wall hanging representing Sun inside the house, through which the family flowed in waves of generations, laughing and chattering, revolving around her quiet and solid presence. They seemed to be in perpetual unhurried motion, feeding in shifts from a table far too small for all that was laden with bowls of corn, beans, and other vegetables, or hauling the great butts of water, solemn for once lest they spill one precious drop ("water is life").

The son and I had long discussions about religion, morality, materialism, and reverence for the processes of life itself; he was interested in hearing about our pre-Christian traditions of solstice ceremonies, the triple goddess, the Green Man, and May Day, and the attempts at reviving them.

"We pray," he said once, "not just for ourselves, our rainfall, our crops, but for you, for everyone out there, for the world."

"But it gets more difficult," the old lady said. "The television doesn't help. It teaches greed and violence, even to our children. And they lose the language." There is no written Hopi language: each village speaks a different dialect, and they cannot agree which should be the official one.

One evening we left them and took an old path down the cliffs, slithering between the rocky ramparts where the son showed us, and following our noses down a steep canyon. Tiny strips of corn dotted terraces carved from precipices, and there were small, twisted fruit trees. As we dropped we could smell the cool of a wash, and after skirting black chasms and skiing down rocky slides, wound down its serpentine coils for miles, twisting and turning in the dark.

We could not leave it, for every traversable patch of dust grew corn. As a shortcut it was a disaster, making an hour's journey into six; but there was no hurry, this was Hopi. From between the walls of the ever-deepening wash, as we jogged along on smooth sand, a corridor of stars blazed overhead.

The boys came again one night, inviting us to their den in an old building up the wash. They played us heavy metal music, which seemed totally out of tune with their attitudes, but they said it was the only music the reservations' pop radio played, and they knew no other. They taught us a game: place a tall glass of beer in the center of a table, take a coin between thumb and middle finger, edge-on, and, with the heel of your hand resting on the table, jerk your hand down hard so that the coin flies up and into the glass. It is not easy. Whoever manages it wins the glass of beer. The first he must drink himself (I liked the way they said that, as if it were a disagreeable penance); after that, he may give anything he wins to whomever he chooses. There were several of us, one from Zuni Pueblo in New Mexico, with a massive, handsome, un-Hopi head. Whether from politeness or teasing, they invariably chose me as the first, and often the only, recipient of their winnings. There was no getting out of it, and there was a lot of beer. I ended up crawling down the wash under revolving galaxies.

Gordon had encouraged us to visit the primary school, but it was closed for Columbus Day, a national holiday when Indians, as they informed us with poker faces, are expected to celebrate being discovered. To mark it, I found an all-American football bug, with a tiny armored head and vast hunched shoulders, striped in scarlet and black. We also found a schoolteacher with rather the same look, and over barbecued chicken, which he prepared in a state of high agitation lest it be less than perfect, we discussed teaching Hopi. He said teachers were encouraged simply to fulfill the curriculum, without any acknowledgment of their beliefs. His wife was part Cree, part Oneida, and of the Bear clan, which is the father of all clans. The major clans, she said, transcended tribal differences, so that the Bear clan on Second Mesa had welcomed her as a sister. "I was brought up with no knowledge of my heritage," she said. "It's like finding you're a member of a family you didn't know existed."

Hearing I was a writer, the teacher showed me a schoolbook aimed at teaching nine-year-olds Creative Writing. Before embarking on a story, you had to draw up a list of *dramatis personae*, describe their characters and their relationships, then formulate the plot structure. Couched in terms that no nine-year-old could possibly understand, it was

the all-American football bug

punctuated with imperatives and strictures guaranteed to ensure complete loss of that wild inventiveness that vitalizes children's writing. It depressed me.

"Would you take this class for me?"

"Gosh. I'm not a teacher."

"No, but you've written novels: this must be second nature to you."

"Er, well, um, we don't all work quite like this." My characters are anarchic. Unmanageable as wild goats, they skip over any attempts to direct them, develop unscheduled conversations, tastes, and obsessions, and produce relatives and friends from murky pasts without anything to do with me. It is hard keeping up with them. It was interesting to find out how it should be done. "If you really want them to work like this, I'll give it a go."

They were very subdued, desks arranged in a U-shape, hands before them in an attitude of obedience. Rick and I did our swinging-lead act about Wales, rain, and our journey, and after lunch we started the story.

"First," I said, feeling a fraud, "we have to work out who we want in this story."

Silence. From what little we had seen of American teaching, it was a one-way process. Teacher taught, and you shut up. Getting them to offer anything proved almost impossible, despite encouragement and plenty of time.

Finally, one said: "Do you think we could have—" and dissolved into shy giggles, rolling his eyes.

"It's okay: whatever you suggest we can all decide on, because this is *our* story."

"Then could we have you?"

"Me?"

"You and your friend and your horses."

This met with general approval, and I wrote it down. Finding another suggestion took another age.

"Could we have a monster with white slimy eyeballs?"

Delighted laughter.

"Sure, if you want a monster with white slimy eyeballs. I'm not sure how the horses will like him, but here we go."

Imagination at last? A Hopi spook? But when the teacher managed to stop laughing, he said: "They had him in a story I read them, and they liked him." Oh. Damn.

The third suggestion, from a big, lively boy, seemed an improvement.

"Could we have a bear?" His eyes slid slyly around the class. Dead silence.

"Good, yes, we'll have a bear."

But why were they now so intent, so breathless with excitement? Suddenly the suggestions poured out, so fast I barely had time to write them down.

"Then can we have a badger?"

"A buck?"

"A butterfly?"

"A rainbow?"

A *rainbow?* Whoever had a rainbow as a character? But

with that strange shift of plane that the Hopi kept giving us, I knew. I wrote down the fifth of the clans they were naming. What were we getting into? The teacher had told me they avoided Hopi culture. I glanced at him but he, feet on his table, seemed oblivious.

"Sun!"

"Eagle!"

"Us!"

The excitement was terrific.

"We're getting rather a lot now," I said carefully, "and we might have difficulty fitting them all in. D'you think Rick and I are in the same story?"

"Maybe not at the beginning," they said, "but maybe later on. There could be more things, too; we'll tell you."

But we only had time for part of it, for explanations about grammar and style held us up. By now they were in full flow, and in such accord that sometimes several of them made the same suggestion at once.

"Once upon a time a bear lived in a canyon," they dictated. "Nearby, in a cave, lived a bad monster. He had white slimy eyeballs. One day the monster decided to eat the bear."

Oh dear. Television-induced violence? But no:

"The monster went to attack the bear, but instead it was the bear that ate the monster, whole. Straightaway he began to feel awful." Of course Bear, having taken it upon himself, as befitted his clan, to absorb this external threat, was bound to suffer ill effects.

"He howled. 'Rrraagh!' he roared."

"'Owwrrraaagh!' he bellowed."

"'*Rrroowwrraaaow!*' he howled."

"A buck and a badger were playing together in a meadow on the edge of the canyon. 'What's that?' they said when they heard the echo of his roars rolling down the canyon. 'Someone's in trouble. Let's go help.'"

No hesitation about this; and who else should help but Badger, who knows medicine, and Antelope, whose horns grow from the top of his head, the center with which he communicates with the Creator? Physical and spiritual help were at hand for Bear.

"When they reached the bear, he was rolling on the ground in agony. They said—"

The bell rang.

"Can we go on with it next time, please, sir?"

"They sure like this Creative Writing," he said, shaking his head in wonder. "Got 'em real fired up." But I was not to know the end of the story.

We helped Perry Honani bury a cow in the wash. She had swollen up so that her legs stuck out like spines from a sea urchin, and we ended up burying the tractor instead, then almost foundering the one we brought to haul it out. I had visions of the whole machinery of Hopi stranded in the wash below a ballooning cow.

He asked if we would like a drive to Tuba City, a Navajo town to the west. We passed the huddle of Oraibi, innocent of wires and television aerials, and swung over the barren mesa-top, where half Navajoland spread out below us in delicate shades of pink and gold. On the other side rose the dark bulk of Coal Mesa, whose mines, despite being in the land the Hopi claim as theirs, are Navajo owned and run.

Surprisingly, Perry had been a Marine during the war, a frontgunner on a landing craft at Iwo Jima and one of the few to escape the slaughter. Many Hopi were conscientious objectors, though those who fought, like the Navajo and other Indians, were renowned for their mad courage in the Pacific war. It was the Navajo, too, who suggested the one radio code that completely foxed the Japanese: their own language.

Tuba City was not an exciting town. Perry said that on this part of the reservation, but especially at Shiprock, too, spiritualism and black magic were rife as people lost faith in the old religion (for he regarded the Navajo religion as a kind of watered-down Hopi without the legendary history. "Navajo are nomads: they go from place to place picking from others."). Many Indians, both Navajo and Hopi, regarded this general loss of faith as being responsible for the poor rainfall in the last few years, which has decimated the already low productivity of the land; or, looked at from another direction, it is our increasingly artificial lifestyle that contributes to changing weather patterns due to global warming.

What is the position of a barren woman in a matriarchal society where female fertility is so revered?

It was not until our third or fourth attempt that we managed to track down the man in Shipaulovi who could tell us where the maze was. He was a highly cultured man who had spent many years in Europe before returning home. It was necessary, he said: going away clarified what was unique and valuable in the Hopi way of life, and forever looking inward and burying one's head in the sands of tradition was impossible. "Hopi must go forward; but uniting in the way to do it is difficult."

We jogged along the top of the mesa toward the medicine man's house. Again Duchess stopped abruptly at the big boulder, gazing at it intently.

"It's got to be near now," Rick said. "It's on a rock half a mile out of the village, he said." We looked around, baffled by the plethora of possible rocks, and it was a while before we thought to wonder what Duchess was staring at.

It was a carving, little more than a hand's breadth across, eroded by the winds of years, but unmistakable. There were no others, only our maze. In its spiraling curves I fancied I could see us, two tiny figures on horseback, trotting through deserts and forests, up cliffs and down canyons, over the wide range and the mesas, into the abyss and back. I finally began to get an inkling of what had happened to us, and to understand from the depths of my emotional being that it is in the acceptance of pain and suffering that we can transcend it, leave it behind, cease to want to defend ourselves by standing truth on its head in blaming and raging; that we can move onward, accepting and finding acceptance, in peace. There is no way to make the process as easy as the words; nor can you direct it. If you keep the top of your head open, your feet find the path.

Rick, with a beatific smile, sat caressing Duchess's mane. Behind them, the gold of the great plain reddened as another cycle drew to a close, and the dust devils began to spin in the evening breeze.

It is a Navajo war god who sings as he rides:

> Before me peaceful,
> Behind me peaceful,
> Under me peaceful,
> Over me peaceful,
> All around me peaceful;
> Peaceful voice when he neighs.
> I am everlasting and peaceful.
> I stand for my horse.

epilogue

STARR CAME TO PICK us up. We were in a different world, dreamy and peaceful, and it took a while to get back into normal ways of speaking, like digging out winter clothes after a summer of nakedness.

We dropped Rosie off at Saartje's in the dark; Duchess, who had shown no signs of even acknowledging her presence, screamed neigh after neigh when she had gone. Horses are forever being ripped from their friends. I did not mind leaving Rosie there, for I knew she would be in the best of homes, but parting from her was hard. With her snorts and puffs, her puppyish affection, her neat ears and her perpetual astonishments, she was a lovable little horse. In a way, I feel I could have done more for her: I had often been more interested in Duchess's antics and progress than in hers. But she managed to find wisdom on the wayside.

Duchess, too, found a good home: with a girl at a boarding school, where she would be ridden under supervision in conditions she would come to know and trust. Rick was shattered. He loved that horse, and had struggled to overcome himself in nurturing her gentle spirit. They had taught each other how to rise above self-protective fear, and what peace is to be won. I tried to remind him that he had saved her, given her trust and a future, but he still felt like a traitor.

Two days later we were in London, dizzied by stinking streets in a dash to a hospital. I sat with our dusty saddlebags while they x-rayed Rick's chest. They said that what had happened in Hopi was clear: his left lung had collapsed completely and suddenly, possibly in delayed reaction to his fall weeks earlier. It was now reflated to nearly eighty percent of its normal extent. The rest would come gradually, without further treatment; it took weeks.

"But whoever treated you in America did a good job to get you that much so fast," they said. "It generally takes major surgery. What did they do?" And were struck dumb.

That whole journey had been made on borrowed time. The question that had been bothering me, Why did he collapse there?, became inverted. Why not before?

The Atlantic swell surges into the entrance of a narrow ravine, its clear waters forcing through the rocks to meet a small trickling stream. The power and rhythm of its boiling upheaval, the slow sucking back, the rise and smash again, are mesmeric, timeless, stripping you of personality into glassy-eyed meditation. A path leads through the trees up the ravine where, on a rock overhung with ivy, are two identical carvings. A hand's breadth across, clear despite the passage of time, unmistakable. There are no other carvings.

Rick and I knelt side by side, tracing them; and below my fingertip I fancied I could see those minuscule figures on horseback, trotting, trotting. But when I got to the middle, I was shaken by a jolt as of lightning, a feeling of terrifying intimacy. For I saw that it was a symbol not only, as the books had told me, of pathways, of emergence and rebirth, of the four directions we must travel, or even of the child wrapped in its protective layers within the womb; but of a phallus within all those layers of alienation with which we women defend ourselves and into which we seldom allow men: the true union of male and female, boundaries merging to form an integrated whole, the act of creation itself.